精彩

Splendid

⊙ 望 野 编著

文物出版社

中原地区宋金之际的民间
彩瓷是很值得重视的
新资料

宿白
七八五年

這批彩瓷都發現在宋金之際
的中小城市中，商品氣息濃厚，
生活情趣盎然，值得重視，是歷史
文獻内不易找到的新史料。

徐苹芳 二〇〇三年七月
於北京

Preface

Shenzhen Wangye Museum which has been approved by the Guangdong Province Cultural Department has been set up in February, 2009, as a newly private museum, prepare this "Splendid·China—A.D. 12-13 Century Decorative Porcelain's Magnificent" exhibition when the founding of the museum, is designed to bring the high-class art enjoyment for citizens of Shenzhen, that is most gratifying.

The colored drawing ceramics of A.D. 12-13 Century, namely, the decorative porcelain of Song and Jin generally spoken, it was popularly called the "Red-green Color" because it was decorated with two colors the red and green. According to statistics, looked from the publications by public or private museums at home and broad nowadays, its collection total quantity not more than one hundred. This exhibition will exhibit 220 pieces (groups) of red-green color ceramics which were collected by the young scholar Yan Yan in Shenzhen, it is the most important rare collections of red-green color ceramics all over the world, so many quantities and varieties and superior qualities that it is unequaled in any other collections of red-green color ceramics.

2009 is the celebration of the 60th anniversary of the founding of New China. The sixty years is a cycle, our great motherland from decay become prosperity and revival. On this happy occasion, use these collections of Wangye Museum to hereby hold this "Splendid·China" exhibition, by the fine peerless red-green color ceramics, to show the culture elegant demeanor and the open verve of Shenzhen who is the city of migrants, and also to wish our motherland stronger and more prosperous.

Real beauty cannot be described by words, records sincerely for the foreword.

Wang Jingsheng
August 31, 2009

序

　　深圳望野博物馆于2009年2月由广东省文化厅批准设立，作为一家新成立的私人博物馆，开馆伊始即筹办《精彩·中国——公元12-13世纪彩瓷的辉煌》展览，旨在为深圳市民带来高品位的艺术享受，可喜可贺。

　　12-13世纪彩绘陶瓷，即通常所说的宋金彩瓷，因其釉面装饰色彩多见红、绿两色，所以俗称"红绿彩"。据统计，从现今海内外公私博物馆公开发表的收藏著录看，其收藏总量不足百件。本次展览共展出红绿彩瓷器220件（组），是目前世界范围内已知最重要的一批红绿彩瓷器珍藏，全部藏品来自深圳青年学者阎焰的收藏，其数量、品种之多，质量之高，是海内外红绿彩瓷器收藏所不能比拟的。

　　2009年，是新中国成立六十周年的大庆。六十年一个甲子，我们伟大的祖国由百废待兴一步步走向繁荣复兴。值此万众欢欣的时节，籍望野博物馆的收藏，特举办《精彩·中国》大展，以精美绝伦的红绿彩瓷器，向世人展现了深圳这座移民城市的文化风采和海纳百川的气魄，也祝愿祖国更加繁荣富强。

　　大美无言，谨记为序。

中共深圳市委宣传部部长

2009. 8. 31

Foreword

Among the Tz'u-chou type wares, enamel painted wares is the most characteristic artifact. It is widely adored by people for its free and elegant brush work, glamorous color and unruly style. The early enamel painted wares is treasured by international collectors because of its limited number.

Archaeological finding indicates that enamel painted wares began to appear in the kilns in Henan, Hebei, Shanxi and Shangdong no late than 12th century. It was the beginning of human using polychrome decorations on the ceramic glaze. From then on, the development of ceramics stepped into a colorful time.

In recent twenty years, a large number of early polychrome overglaze decoration ceramics had been dug out in the large-scale old-city reform of north China area (where are often the sites of ancient cites). The quantity and quality, the richness of their variety, and the vast areas of their spread and use are all unprecedented as long as the academic circle knows. These materials proved that the polychrome overglaze decoration ceramics had already reached a peak as early as A.D. 12 to 13 centuries. Its artistic value is comparable to that Kang, Yong and Qian periods of Qing Dynasty, which is known as the golden age of the Chinese ancient colored drawing ceramics.

The historical reason of the prosperity of polychrome overglaze decoration ceramics was multiple: the longtime stability of the political situation of northern China, the boom of urban commercial economy and the growth of street culture. It was also the fruit of cultural colliding and mingling of the wild and simple grassland culture and the middle land culture which values elegance and reserve.

These ceramics carried with them a lot of information concerning the social life then, such as secular and religious life, paintings of flowers, birds and human figures, decorative calligraphy of verse, pottery human figures for display, etc. These materials undoubtedly will be a brand new information source of Song and Jin dynasties history research and urban life research.

These polychrome overglaze decoration ceramics not only inaugurated the Chinese overglaze decoration, and enriched the aesthetic field of Chinese ceramics, and also made far-reaching influence on later era of china and the world ceramic art history. In the remote 12th century, Chinese people painted the first brush on the ceramics, just like an extraordinary rainbow.

前 言

在磁州窑类型瓷器当中，红绿彩是最具特色的产品之一。它以鲜艳靓丽的色彩，自由飘逸的画法，豪放洒脱的风格深受世人喜爱。早期红绿彩瓷器，因传世和出土器物有限，更被海内外视若珍藏。

考古资料表明，至迟在公元12世纪末的河南、河北、山西、山东等地窑场，已出现在釉面上描绘绚丽色彩的红绿彩瓷器。它是人类在瓷器釉面上使用多种色彩装饰的开始。从此，瓷器的发展进入了一个五彩缤纷的时代。

近二十年来，中国华北地区大规模的旧城改造中陆续发现了大量早期红绿彩瓷器。其数量之大，品质之高，种类之多，流传使用范围之广，为此前学界所不知。最新的资料表明，早在公元12-13世纪，中国的釉上彩绘瓷器就已经达到了一个空前的高度。其艺术成就，即使与号称中国古代彩绘瓷黄金时代的清，康、雍、乾三朝相比亦毫不逊色。

早期红绿彩瓷器的兴盛，是在中国北方政局长期稳定、城市商品经济持续繁荣、市井文化高度发达的历史背景下，豪放粗犷、崇真尚实、以俗为美、清新质朴的草原文明与崇尚平淡高雅，温柔内敛的中原文化碰撞、交融的结果。

这些红绿彩瓷器中存储了当时中国封建社会中市民生活的大量信息，诸如各类世俗宗教题材，花鸟人物绘画，书法诗词装饰，人物陈列摆设等不一而足。这些信息的保留无疑将成为研究宋金历史及当时社会生活的珍贵资料。

红绿彩瓷器不仅开创了中国釉上彩装饰的先河，极大地丰富了中国陶瓷的审美领域，而且对后世中国乃至世界陶瓷釉上彩瓷的发展都产生了广泛而深远的影响。遥远的12世纪前后中国人首次在瓷器上描绘出的绚丽色彩，宛如一道彩虹，令人叹为观止。

目　录

CONTENTS

1、释迦牟尼像

12—13世纪
高34.8厘米

胎色灰黄，模制中空，施化妆土，罩透明釉，内底无釉露胎，中心部位有透气孔。造型为佛祖本尊结跏趺坐于须弥座的莲台之上，莲台红彩勾描，须弥座红绿黄彩间隔装饰，中有开光红彩绘花，背后无彩。佛结"法界定印"，脸圆额满，眉目庄严，唇上撇胡，下巴颏处有螺旋线样胡髯。面、肤无衣饰遮处尽为亮黄色，头顶有螺旋肉髻，黑彩涂绿釉装饰，绿釉多剥蚀。肉髻隆起，状如积粟覆瓯，此相名"无见顶相"。在肉髻与额间有红色髻珠，此种髻珠形制样式，多出现于唐代，随时代以降，越来越大，五代至宋季，成为佛发的重要组成部分。《大慈恩寺三藏法师传》载僧伽罗国王宫侧有金像"髻有宝珠，无知其价"。佛体着五衣，红色为主调，绿边。内有衷衣"安陀会"，画水纹，身穿绿色"郁多罗"，袖边绘曲折花；外罩"僧伽黎"；肩披"僧祇支"、下身"涅槃僧"，皆红色点绘黄蔓草花。《弘明集》载汉末牟融《理惑论》："今沙门被赤布"，可知佛教东传后，释子袈裟用红为主色，是为常例，近两千年未改。

1. The Sakyamuni figurine

The 12-13th century
Height 34.8cm

The figurine is moulding and hollow, color of its figuline is lark, daubed the dressing-clay on its body, and covered with transparent glaze, the inner foot hasn't glaze to bare the roughcast, and middle of it has an air-hole. The figure of this figurine was modeled on the Sakyamuni, this Buddha sits cross-legged on lotus throne of the Xumizuo (the pedestal of a statue of Buddha)), the lotus throne was delineated with red color. The front of Xumizuo was decorated with red, green and yellow colors, middle of which there have patterns that are red flower in red circle on white background, but the back no colors. The Buddha made a "Fa Jie Ding Yin (Sanskrit is Samadhimudra, one of the Buddhist gesture)", round face and plump forehead, stately brows and eyes, moustaches over the mouth, and on the chin there has a helical beard. His face and bare skin which are all bright yellow, there have many helical fleshy-buns on his head which were delineated with black color and applied green glaze, most green glaze had faded. The apophysis of fleshy-buns which look like cumulate millet, this style that be called "Wu Jian Ding Xiang (means can't see the calvaria of Buddha, one of the Buddha's looks)". There has a red bead in fleshy-buns, this style of bead that appeared most at Tang Dynasty, the bead became bigger and bigger along with times passed, it had become the important part of the Buddha's hairstyle from the Five Dynasties to Song Dynasty. It is recorded by DA CI EN SI SAN ZANG FA SHI ZHUAN (THE BIOGRAPHY OF MONK SAN ZANG OF BIG CIEN TEMPLE) that there has one gold sculpture which is "precious bead in bun, invaluable treasure" at the side of the palace of Seng Jia Luo (Sanskrit is Simhalauipa) Kingdom (the name for the old Sri Lanka). This Buddha wares the Five Cīvara (the monk's cloth), the main color is red, green border. The inner have underclothing "An Tuo Hui (Sanskrit is Antaravāsaka)", painted ripple, wares green "Yu Duo Luo (Sanskrit is Uttarāsanga)", painted flowers on sleeves' border, wares "Seng Jia Li (Sanskrit is Sanghāti)", drapes "Seng Zhi Zhi (Sanskrit is Sankaksikā)" over his shoulders, and wares "Nie Pan Seng (Sanskrit is Nivasana)", painted yellow vines. LI HUO LUN (UNDERSTANDING OF BUDDHISM) written by Mou Rong in the Late Han Dynasty which in HONG MING JI (the collected works of Buddhism) said: "The Buddhist monks all ware red today", after the Buddhism was transmitted eastward, it has been the usual that the main color of cassock is red, and never changed for two thousand years.

2、手指白云弥勒像

12—13世纪
高35.6厘米

　　胎色灰，模制中空，施化妆土，罩透明釉，器底有透气孔。弥勒右手竖臂遥指，赤足立于四方台之上，方台分三层，最底层正面壶门彩绘，壶门外满涂红彩，壶门内釉下黑彩绘蔓草花上涂绿彩，两侧黑彩画壶门，外涂红彩，背面白地黑彩画壶门无彩绘；第二层，黑彩勾边，正面及两侧满绘绿彩，背后留白；最上一层黑红彩间隔勾线，白地黑彩书"手指白云弥勒"。佛头大而圆，双耳垂肩，满面喜乐，额顶有突起肉髻，两腮两个肉窝，双下巴，肥胖无颈，口大张，唇红齿白；体态丰满，袒胸露腹，胸前戴佛珠，制式明确，红珠黄心，珠与珠间有三颗黑隔珠。僧袍红色广袖，肩袖上有黄色云草纹，领口绿彩黄红圈花，袖口绿彩黑蔓草花；外罩黄边绿色"郁多罗"，由七块红地淡绿色蔓草方片补缀成衣，左后背靠肩处有环襻扣带。下身"涅槃僧"，黑色有花褶。左手垂于侧前，紧握一黄布口袋，口袋上有黑彩点描出针脚效果的两块方、圆补丁。所有袒露肌肤处都用粉色涂染，表现出肉质感，生动传神。此像最特殊处是有自铭。弥勒，是梵文"Maitreya"的音译，意译为"慈氏"，是佛教中的菩萨名，最早出现于《阿含经》中。弥勒信仰随佛教东传入中国，一度盛行，经典中多有记载，竺法护译《弥勒下生经》、鸠摩罗什译《弥勒成佛经》、沮渠京声译《观弥勒菩萨上生兜率天经》，号称"弥勒三部经"。因"弥勒下生"之由，自北魏中期以后，历代农民常借此为口号造反起义。甚至武曌以周代唐，也用"弥勒下生"作文章。弥勒，先于世尊入灭，将在未来世界接替继承释迦牟尼的佛位，其被思变的民众和利益集团直接政治借用，这在佛教中也算是一个特例。

2. A Maitreya whose finger points to the cloud figurine

The 12-13th century
Height 35.6cm

　　The figurine is moulding and hollow, color of its figuline is gray, daubed the dressing-clay on its body, and covered with transparent glaze, it has an air-hole on the bottom. Maitreya puts his right arm up to point to the distance, stands on a quadrate support, which with three layers, the floor, on which facade it was painted kunmen (a purfle pattern whose shape like doorframe), in which it was painted the twiner with black color and then spread green color on, and painted red color out of the kunmen, two sides of the floor were painted kunmen with black color, out of it was painted red color, back of the floor was painted black kunmen on white background without colored pattern; the second layer, delineated the black line, the facade and two sides were spread green color, but the back is white; top layer, delineated the black and red lines, calligraphed the Chinese characters "Shou Zhi Bai Yun Mi Le" on the white background. This Buddha, whose head is big and round, ears droop to the shoulders, happy countenance, there has a fleshy-bun, two dimples, double chin, fat and no neck, open mouth, red lips and white teeth; plump posture, exposes his chest and belly, wears Buddhist beads, standard model, red bead with yellow core, three black beads partition. The frock is red and with large sleeves, on the sleeves and shoulders there have yellow patterns, neckline has yellow and red flowers with the green background, cuffs have black tendril patterns with green background; wears green "Yu Duo Luo (Uttarāsanga)" with yellow border, which were patched by seven pieces of quadrate material whose pattern are red background pea green tendrils, and there has a loop to buckle the belt at his left back. Wears "Nie Pan Seng (Nivasana)", black with pleats. The left hand holds a yellow sack, on which there has quadrate and round patches which are painted with black color. All bare skin was dyed with nude pink to show the color of skin, it is vivid and lively. It is especial that has the epigraph. Mi Le, it is the transliteration of the Sanskrit "Maitreya", paraphrase is "Family of Mercy", it is the name of Bodhisattva at Buddhism, which appears the earliest in AGAMASUTRA. The Maitreya Faith along with the Buddhism was introduced into China, it was once common, it has many recordations in classics, THE MI LE XIA SHENG JING (ONE OF THE PRINCIPAL SCRIPTURES FOR THE CULT OF MAITREYA) translated by Zhufahu (Dharmaraksa), THE MI LE CHEGN FO JING (THE SUTRA OF MAITREYA BECOMING BUDDHA) translated by Jiumoluoshi (Kumarajiva), GUAN MI LE PU SA SHANG SHENG DOU SHUAI TIAN JING (Maitreya) translated by Juqujingsheng, that are called "the three scriptures of Maitreya". Cause the reason of "the Maitreya was born", the farmer always revolted after the middle of Northern Wei. The Wu Zhao (Wu Zetian) supplanted the Zhou Dynasty by Tang Dynasty, even also used the reason of "the Maitreya was born". Maitreya, who was Rumie (dead, parin!irvati) before Sakyamuni, and would inherit the place of Sakyamuni in the future world, it is a special case in the Buddhism that which was borrowed by plebs and Interest Groups.

3、弥勒佛像

12—13世纪
高22.5厘米

　　胎色灰黄，模制中空，施化妆土，通体罩透明釉，底部无釉露胎，有透气孔。造型为一弥勒袒胸露腹坐于石台上，石台黑彩勾涂。弥勒，头圆面阔，双耳垂肩，两腮两个肉窝，肥胖无颈，唇舌殷红；体态丰满，袒胸露腹，胸前戴佛珠，红线绳串绿珠。红袈裟，上画绿彩云草纹，袖边领口绿彩涂染，左肩头有环襻扣带。左手抚膝，右手置于腹前手拈绿色佛珠，脚蹬黑鞋，身左腰间挂有一黄色口袋。弥勒信仰在民间一直都有流行，中世纪以后开始出现袒胸露腹，笑口常开的"大肚弥勒佛"，这一造型不同于唐以前的样式，此民间化的"大肚弥勒佛"的原型来自——布袋和尚。《宋人轶事汇编》载，五代后梁（907年——923年）间，浙江奉化有一僧："身矮而腹皤，尝负一口袋，人目为'布袋和尚'"。《梁高僧传》、《五灯会元》、《二浙名贤录》记此僧名叫"契此"，并多录有其洞知未来，了明吉凶的轶闻趣事。后梁贞明三年（917年），布袋和尚在奉化岳林寺东廊石凳上无疾趺化，葬城北封山（今锦屏山）的中塔，后人传称见其显身各处，灵异连连，还得其偈语"弥勒真弥勒，化身千百亿。时时示世人，世人自不识"。从此各庙宇佛寺，都以布袋和尚为弥勒化身，塑形，成为汉地佛教最为世人所熟知喜奉的佛像之一，广受香火。《宋高僧传》载："江浙之间多图画其像"。杭州飞来峰崖壁上就有宋人雕刻的大肚布袋弥勒像。

3. Buddha Maitreya figurine

The 12-13th century
Height 35.6cm

　　The figurine is moulding and hollow, color of its figuline is lark, daubed the dressing-clay on its body, and covered with transparent glaze, the foot hasn't glaze to bare the roughcast, and an air-hole on it. The visual shape that is a Maitreya sits on the stone support and exposes his chest and belly, the stone support was daubed with black color. The Maitreya, who has round head and wide face, ears droop to the shoulders, two dimples, fat and no neck, lips and tongue are all red; plump posture, exposes his chest and belly, wears Buddhist beads which are yellow beads that were strung with red rope together. Red cassock, which was painted green patterns, the cuffs and neckline were daubed with green color, it has a loop to buckle the belt at his left back. The left hand presses knee, right hand picks up the green Buddhist beads at the front of belly, wears black shoes on feet, a yellow sack at his left waist. The Maitreya Faith has prevailed in the folk, the "large belly Buddha Maitreya", who has a beam of delight and exposes his chest and belly, has begun to arise after middle ages, this visual shape is differ from the modality which before Tang Dynasty, the prototype of this folk "large belly Buddha Maitreya" comes from the Monk Budai (with a sack). It was recorded by SONG REN YI SHI HUI BIAN (COMPILATION OF ANECDOTES OF SONG PERSONALITIES) that there has a monk in Fenghua Zhejiang at the period of the Posterior Liang Dynasty (A.D.907-923), "runty and big-bellied, always carried a sack, was called 'Monk Budai'". THE LIANG GAO SENG ZHUAN (BIOGRAPHY OF ACCOMPLISHED MONK LIANG DYNASTY), WU DENG HUI YUAN, ER ZHE MING XIAN LU, which recorded this monk's name is "Qi Ci" who can see the future and know the good or ill luck. The third year of Zhenming the Posterior Liang Dynasty (A.D. 917), the Monk Budai died on stone stool which in the east corridor of Yuelin Temple Fenghua, was buried in middle pagoda in Mount Feng at north city, the later generations alleged that they saw this Monk show his presence everywhere, such the spectral things appeared repeatedly, and get the Buddhist's words "True Maitreya who has thousands upon thousands incarnations. Always show his presence to earthling, but nobody knows." Hence, every shrine and temple used the Monk Budai for the incarnation of Maitreya to figure, it became one of the joss which is known and dedicated to by earthling in Chinese Buddhism. It was recorded by BIOGRAPHY OF SONG ACCOMPLISHED MONK that "Its portrait was painted more at Jianshu and Zhejiang area". The cliffside of the Peak Flying at Hangzhou, where has the portrait of large belly Budai Maitreya which was carved at Song Dynasty.

4-1、牵狮俑座

12—13世纪
高20.6厘米　　宽22.4厘米

　　胎灰黄色较酥松，模制中空，施化妆土，罩透明釉，有细碎开片。狮子披带绿云头装饰的红鞍（红彩脱落，仅有很少残留），驮一圆台，黑彩绘眉、眼、鼻、嘴、鬃毛、须等，绿彩涂绘头、皮肤，黄彩染绘鬃毛和尾毛，身下有模印的卷云纹。身前有一控狮人，面向左，短髭、桃形须，戴黑盔，穿紧身圆领袍，内衣绿领，胸前抹绿花，扎黄胸带，腰系"抱肚"，蹬靴。右手牵拉系在狮颈部项圈上的长索，索穿过肩部垂下由左手紧拽。这导致狮头微侧，双目向拉系索方向斜视。狮子张开血盆大口，双目圆睁，瞳仁下视，造型生动，神采飞扬，多处红彩已剥落，绿、黄彩鲜艳。此造型在大足石刻和山西的庙宇泥塑等宗教图像中都有，名为"青狮"，是中国佛教里"文殊菩萨"的坐骑。同样式的制品，1972年河北邯郸的峰峰矿区有窖藏出土（见：秦大树　李喜仁　马忠理：《邯郸市峰峰矿区出土的两批红绿彩瓷器》，《文物》1997年　第10期，P32页，封底图3），台湾"华艺轩"也有收藏（见：香港《中国文物世界》1995年1月号，总113期）。其中峰峰矿区窖藏出土的无论釉彩和工艺造型，要远逊色于这件，可确认烧造时间较晚。而台湾所藏和这件则非常相似，宛如同模，可惜是脱彩严重。就目前之发现研究，此一铺多尊的成套宗教供像，当时的制作量较大，应是在某一地烧好坯后，分散运到临近各销售地烤花加彩的。

4-1. The pulled lion figurine pedestal

The 12-13th century
Height 20.6cm, Width 22.4cm

　　Yellow figuline is loose, the hollow figurine is moulding, daubed the body with dressing-clay, and then covered with transparent glaze on which it has finely-broken clastic grains. The lion is draped a red saddle decorated with green cloud-heads (the red color was shed, only have little color residue), carried one round stand on its back, the eyebrows, eyes, nose, lips, mane and beard were painted with black color, painted head and skin with green color, dyed mane and cercus yellow, stamped winding-cloud patterns under its body. One man, who controls the lion at the front of lion, face to the left, short mustache and peach-shape beard, wears black helmet on his head, pulls on succinct gown with round collar, undergarment has green collar, painted green flower at the bosom, ties a yellow chest strap, and ties "Bao Du" on his waist, wears boots. The man pulls the large halter which tied the collar of the lion's neck with his right hand, the halter across his shoulder, which was held tightly by his left hand. It makes the lion's head inclined towards the left, both eyes squint the direction where is the man standing. The lion is opening its big bloody mouth, opening eyes round-eyed, pupils of the eyes looking down, moulding lifelikeness, glowing in high spirit, many red colors have exfoliated, but green and yellow colors are still bright-colored. This moulding also in the religionary images of Dazu caved stone and Shanxi's clay sculpture, name is "Qing Shi (Green Lion)", which is the beast for riding of the "Bodhisattva Wen Shu" in Chinese Buddhism. The same ware which has been unearthed from the hoard of Fengfeng mining area Handan Hebei at 1972 (see: Qin Dashu, Li Xiren and Ma Zongli, "TWO GROUPS OF RED AND GREEN PORCELAINS UNEARTHED AT FENGFENG MINING AREA HANDAN", WENWU, 10, 1997, p.32, & fig, 3 of back cover), it has also be collected by "Hua Yi Xuan" Taiwan (see: ART OF CHINA, HK, the 113th, Jan, 1995). Of which but the ware of Fengfeng mining area's hoard, it is very inferior to this one from the glaze's color and moulding technology, and it can be affirmed that the time when the ware was fired is later, at later stage of Jin Dynasty approximately. The ware which be collected by Taiwan same as this one, as it were same mold, it is to be regretted that it has serious decolor. From the researches and discoveries at present, the complete set of religionary figurines, had bigger production at that time, it should be fired the semifinished product, and then be carried to each sale-places to add the colors with decorating fire.

4-2、牵象俑座

12—13世纪
高19.2厘米　宽21.3厘米

　　胎灰黄色较酥松，模制中空，施化妆土，罩透明釉，有细碎开片。大象披带绿云头装饰的红鞍，驮一圆台，黑彩绘象眼、索饰等，通体洁白，红彩绘"六牙"，短鼻，长耳，身下有模印的卷云纹。身前有一控象人，面向右，短髭、桃形须，戴黑盔，穿圆领红黄边白袍，肩系绿巾，下身着黄边绿裙系绿巾带，蹬靴。左手牵拉系在狮颈部项圈上的长索，索穿过肩部垂下由右手紧拽，使象头微回弯。象头部有红、黄彩加黑、绿圈的带饰。此象"六牙"，名"六牙白象"，是佛教中的圣物，为"普贤菩萨"的坐骑，同样造型在四川峨眉山和1954年日本京都清凉寺发现北宋雍熙元年（984年）的佛教版画（见：[日]塚本善隆《奝然请到日本的释迦佛像胎内的北宋文物》，《现代佛学》，1957年第11期）及其他宗教图像都可以看到。尤其是日本京都清凉寺发现的版画清晰的描绘了"普贤菩萨"骑"六牙白象"，"文殊菩萨"骑"青狮"的造型。

4-2. The pulled elephant figurine pedestal

The 12-13th century
Height 19.2cm, Width 21.3cm

　　Yellow figuline is loose, the hollow figurine is moulding, daubed the body with dressing-clay, and then covered with transparent glaze on which it has finely-broken clastic grains. The elephant is draped a red saddle decorated with green cloud-heads, carried one round stand on its back, the elephant's eyes, halter, and so on were painted black color, the whole body is whiteness, painted "Liu Ya (six teeth)", short nose, long ears, stamped winding-cloud patterns under its body. One man who controls the elephant at the front of lion, face to the left, short mustache and peach-shape beard, wears black helmet on his head, pulls on round collar white gown with red and yellow borders, ties green shawl on his shoulder, wears green skirt with yellow border and ties green cincture on his waist, wears boots. The man pulls the large halter which tied the collar of the elephant's neck with his left hand, the halter across his shoulder, which was held tightly by his right hand. It makes the elephant's inclines its head. The elephant's head was decorated with band by red, yellow, green and black colors. The elephant is "Liu Ya", called "Liu Ya Bai Xiang (Six-tooth White Elephant), it is the holy beast in the Buddhism, is the beast for riding of the "Bodhisattva Pu Xian", the same model can be seen at Emei Mountain Sichuan, and the Buddhism woodcut of the first year of Yong Xi North Song (A.D. 984) that was found in Qing Liang Temple Kyoto Japan at 1954 (see: Japan, Tsukamoto Zenry, "THE CULTURAL RELICS OF NORTH SONG INNER THE SAKYAMUNI'S STATUE WHICH WAS BROUGHT TO JAPAN BY DIAO RAN", MODERN BUDDHISM, 11, 1957), and others religionary images. In especial, the woodcut which was found in Qing Liang Temple Kyoto Japan, it was portrayed the "Bodhisattva Pu Xian" ridding on the "Liu Ya Bai Xiang" and the "Bodhisattva Wen Shu" ridding on the "Qing Shi" legibly.

5、包髻贵妇像

12—13世纪
高30.8厘米　底台纵长11厘米　宽10.5厘米

　　灰黄色胎，质酥松，模制，施化妆土，罩玻璃釉，色微黄，多细碎开片，底部扎有透气孔。整个造型是一位年轻美丽的妇人坐于椅台上。头部簪花"包髻"，黑彩涂绘表示头发，黑发外蒙一层以绿釉涂抹的纱罗状遮盖物，头后部的包髻巾为红色，发半露。黑彩绘眉眼，红彩点唇，鬓两侧有细细的发绺垂下。身着浅粉色左衽、绿领、绿袖、绿边红绿花的广袖衫，最里面还有红色左衽内衣，仅露领口。脖子上戴有挂饰的金（黄釉）项圈。下身穿红色藤黄花点长裙，裙腰高提，束于胸下，外翻，绿板革带紧扎，交袖抄手，裙前两腿间有黄色红绿蔓草纹"前襈"，足蹬"绿舄"。肩部有绿色红葵花窄幅"披帛"，帛头留于前面被广袖遮盖。椅背后大红色椅裙。恰应了明汤显祖《牡丹亭》第二十七出："翠翘金凤，红裙绿袄，环佩玎珰，敢真仙下降？"的描述。其造型、发饰、衣着和山西晋祠的那些名闻天下的宋代，彩绘泥塑有异曲同工之妙，属极其难得珍贵的金代完整服饰例样。

5. The Bao Ji (one of hairstyle) lady figurine

The 12-13th century
Height 19.2cm, the bottom-stand length 11cm, Width 21.3cm

　　The figuline is lark, texture is loose, moulding, daubed the body with dressing-clay, and then covered with yellowish vitreous glaze, on which it has many finely-broken clastic grains, it was poked an air hole on the bottom. The model which is a young beauteous lady sitting on the chair. Wears flowers in her hair and "Bao Ji" on head, painted black color to show the hair, it has a tier of covering like leno which was painted with green glaze over the black hair, the Bao Ji which at back of head is red, bares the hair half. Drew the eyebrows and eyes with black color, stippled the lips with red color, two thin tufts of hair lolling from the both sides of hair on the temple. Wears mandarin sleeve clothing with front of a garment left which is pale pink, green collar, green sleeve, and green border with red and green flowers, it still has red undergarment with front of a garment left inside, just bares the collar. Gold (yellow glaze) chaplet on her neck. Wears red long skirt stippled yellow flowers, the skirt is tied under the bosom, turned over the skirt's waist outwards, tied tightly by green band, folds her arms in sleeves, it has yellow "Qian Da" which with red and pattern of green twiners between the legs, wears "Green Xi (shoes)" on feet. It has small green "Pi Bo (silk ribbon)" with pattern of red sunflowers on shoulder, the ends of the ribbon is covered by mandarin sleeves. The bright red chair cover. Just like the poem of the MU DAN TING (PEONY PAVILION) described that: "Cui Qiao (the name of jewelry which likes kingfisher's feathers) gold phoenix, red skirt green jacket, jade pendant tinkled, is it possible that the real fairy visits?" which was written by Tang Xianzu of Ming Dynasty. The moulding, topknot, and clothing with those well-known colored drawing clay sculpture of Song Dynasty which are in the Jin Memorial Hall of Shanxi Province, different in approach but equally satisfactory in result, it is the rounded example of dress and personal ornament of Jin Dynasty at 12th century, very valuably.

6、凤冠贵妇像

12—13世纪
高32.1厘米　底台纵长13厘米　宽9.6厘米

灰黄色胎，质酥松，模制，施化妆土，罩玻璃釉，色微黄，多细碎开片，底部扎有透气孔。整个造型是一位年轻貌美雍容华贵的妇人坐于椅台上。头部簪花包髻，博鬓，戴金（黄釉）凤冠，黑彩涂绘表示头发，头后部的包髻巾为红色，发半露，梳鬟。黑彩绘眉眼，红彩点唇，鬟两侧有细细的发绺垂下。身着左衽红色、藤黄点花、绿边的广袖衫，最里面红色左衽内衣，仅露领口。脖子上戴有大花状挂饰的金（黄釉）项圈。下身穿红裙、白裤，裙腰高提，束于胸下，黄板革带紧扎，交袖抄手，裙前绿边红色米字格"蔽膝"盖双腿，有绿色垂绦，足蹬红舄。肩部披黄色红边的"云肩"，外搭绿色红葵花窄幅"披帛"，帛圆带留在前面，帛头后垂被衣衫遮盖。椅背后大朵红绿色花卉椅褡。在广袖半截处，有绿色羽毛状装饰。这种羽饰和凤冠、蔽膝、革带的搭配，都显示了它就应该是《宋史·舆服志》中记载的"褕翟"。这些搭配是12世纪间后妃才能穿着的命妇冠服。它的图样对中国服饰史研究有着极其重要的价值。与此相同的制品，在上海博物馆也收藏有一尊，但遗憾，因上博这尊残损缺失严重，当年在修复中仅凭想象而将衣衽、云肩、项饰做了错误的处理。今天比对这件俑像的图样基本可以重新恢复上博所藏之原貌。这些俑像中出现的"左衽"已决定了它们并非是宋代的制品，尤其是"云肩"属于较常见和广泛使用的女真服饰（见：金代张瑀（据传）绘《文姬归汉图》中骑于马上的文姬装束），它的纹样对后世的服装和其他制品图案化装饰影响深远，在元、明陶瓷纹样中经常出现。

6. The phoenix coronet lady figurine

The 12-13th century
Height 32.1cm, the bottom-stand length 13cm, Width 9.6cm

The figuline is lark, texture is loose, moulding, daubed the body with dressing-clay, and then covered with yellowish vitreous glaze, on which it has many finely-broken clastic grains, it was poked an air hole on the bottom. The model which is a young beauteous lady has supreme elegance sitting on the chair. Wears flowers in her hair and Bao Ji (one of hairstyle) on head, wide sideburns, wears gold (yellow glaze) phoenix coronet, was painted black color to show the hair, he Bao Ji which at back of head is red, bares the hair half, combed hair bun. Drew the eyebrows and eyes with black color, stippled the lips with red color, two thin tufts of hair lolling from the both sides of hair on the temple. Wears mandarin sleeve clothing with front of a garment left which is red, stippled yellow flowers, and green border, it still has red undergarment with front of a garment left inside, just bares the collar. Gold (yellow glaze) chaplet has decorated with big flower on her neck. Wears red skirt and white trousers, waist of skirt is tied under the bosom by yellow leather band tightly, folds arms in sleeves, over the skirt there has "Bi Xi (knee's covering)" which has red asteroid and green border covering the legs, with green silk braid, wears red Xi (shoes) on feet. Drape "Yun Jian (cloud-shape tippet)" which is yellow with red border over shoulder, hangs green "Pi Bo (silk ribbon)" with pattern of red sunflowers over shoulder. It has the chair cover which pattern is big red and green flowers at the chair's back. Decorated the mandarin sleeves with green featheriness. Such feathers decoration collocates with phoenix coronet, Bi Xi, and leather band, all of these demonstrate that it must be the "Yu Di (feathers clothing)" which was recorded in SONG SHI · YU FU ZHI (HISTORY OF SONG RECORD OF VEHICLE CLOTHES AND HAT). The finery collocation is the clothes and hat of Ming Fu (a woman in ancient China who was given a rank by the emperor), that only can be wore by empress and imperial concubines at the 12th century. Its patterns have value of vital importance to make researches on Chinese trappings history. The same figurine which was collected by Shanghai Museum, but it is to be regretted that this one has grievous damage, done the wrong disposal of garment's front, Yun Jian, and sautoir when repaired it. The figurine which was collected by Shanghai Museum can be resumed afresh today, that according to the patterns of this phoenix coronet lady Figurine. The "Zuo Ren (left garment's front)" which pattern on these figurines had been decided that they are not the wares of Song Dynasty, especially, the "Yun Jian" is the familiar raiment of Nuchen used widely (see: the attire of lady Wen who rode on a horse, which was drawn in WENJI GUI HAN TU (DRAWING OF LADY WEN RETURN HAN) by Zhang Yu Jin Dynasty), its patterns had profound and lasting influence upon the decoration of clothing and other wares at later ages, always appeared in ceramics' pattern at Yuan and Ming Dynasty.

7、弈棋仕女像

12—13世纪
高25.8厘米

　　灰黄色胎，质酥松，模制中空，施化妆土，罩玻璃釉，底部有透气孔。整个造型是一位年轻貌美气质高华的仕女坐于花牙鼓凳上。头部红色包髻，髻前三朵圆形花饰，头发用黑彩涂就，微压双耳，发丝及发式轮廓清晰。黑彩绘眉眼，红彩点唇，面颊用粉色晕染。身着左衽绿色黑花长袖衫，领边白地黑花，衷衣红领，下穿红裙黄色点花，腰束绿色丝绦。一条粉色点绿花披帛，从身后穿绕臂间、膝下，帛头垂于腰后两侧。仕女左手托四方黑框红棋盒，绿袖长垂，右手入棋盒拈子。黑彩花牙鼓凳后部半露，前部被裙遮盖，此类家具牙角样式在宋金时期的考古壁画、石刻中多见。英国巴斯（Bath）远东艺术博物馆所藏红绿彩仕女人物像，所坐也是此类花牙凳。

7. Figurine of beauty plays go

The 12-13th century
Height 25.8cm

　　The figurine is moulding and hollow, its figuline is lark and loose, daubed the dressing-clay on its body, covered with vitreous glaze, and it has an air-hole on the bottom. The visual shape is a beauty who is youthful, fair-faced, with noble bearing, sits on a drum shape stool with flowers pattern. Red Baoji (a kerchief, worn as a head covering) on her head, at the fore of which it has three cycloidal floriation, the hair which painted with black color covers ears a little, the hairline and each hair are clear-cut. The eyebrows and eyes were painted with black color, lips were stippled red, and dyed the cheeks incarnadine. Wears green clothing which has long sleeves, black patterns, and the front of the clothing is left, the neckline has black patterns on white background, the underclothing has red collar, wears red skirt with yellow flowers, and ties green silk braid on waist. A pink silk ribbon with green patterns, which was wrapped from the back to arm and knees, lolls from waist to each side at the back. The beauty holds a go-box which is red, square and with black frame in her left palm, long green sleeve lolling, the right hand picks up the piece into the go-box. The drum shape stool which with black Huaya pattern, that was covered the front part by skirt but bared the back part, the Huaya or Yajiao pattern, which are the fashion of Chinese furniture, that can be seen much in the fresco and carved stone of Song and Jin dynasties. The red and green colors beauty figurine which is collected by the Museum of East Asian Art in Bath also has this Huaya stool.

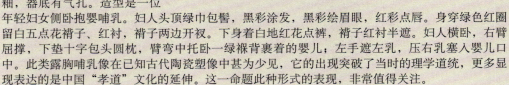

8、哺乳像

12—13世纪
高9.5厘米　长12.2厘米

　　胎色灰黄，模制中空，施化妆土，局部露胎，罩透明釉，器底有气孔。造型是一位年轻妇女侧卧抱婴哺乳。妇人头顶绿巾包髻，黑彩涂发，黑彩绘眉眼，红彩点唇。身穿绿色红圈留白五点花褙子、红衬，褙子两边开衩。下身着白地红花点裤，褙子红衬半遮。妇人横卧，右臂屈撑，下垫十字包头圆枕，臂弯中托卧一绿褓背裹着的婴儿；左手遮左乳，压右乳塞入婴儿口中。此类露胸哺乳像在已知古代陶瓷塑像中甚为少见，它的出现突破了当时的理学道统，更多显现表达的是中国"孝道"文化的延伸。这一命题此种形式的表现，非常值得关注。

8. Figurine of lacting woman

The 12-13th century
Height 9.5cm, length 12.2cm

　　The figurine is moulding and hollow, color of its figuline is lark, daubed the dressing-clay on its body, part of it bared the roughcast, covered with transparent glaze, the bottom has an air-hole. The visual shape that is a young feme lies on her side and suckling her baby. Green Baoji on her head, painted hair with black color, the eyebrows and eyes were painted with black color, lips were stippled red. Wears green short robe which has red patterns, red lining, slits at the sides. Wears white trousers with red flowers, which was covered a half by the red lining of short robe. The feme lies on her right side, bent her right arm to support, and underlaid a roundish pillow which was wrapped the top to be a cross shape, a baby who was wrapped in green swaddle lies in her arm; left hand presses her right nipple into baby's mouth. This kind of figurine which visual shape is a lacting woman bared her breast, it is few in the known archaic ceramic figurine, it surmounted the orthodoxy of Li Xue (Confucian school of idealist philosophy of the Song) at that time, it is the prolongation of Chinese "Xiao Dao (Confucian doctrine of filial piety)" culture which was showed more. Deserve attention very much.

9、和合立像

12—13世纪
高27厘米

胎灰黄色，模制中空，施化妆土，罩透明釉，器底有透气孔。造型为两人攀肩搭背并立于六方台座上，台座壶券，有红绿黄彩点涂，局部黑彩勾线。两人眉目清秀，神态喜乐。左立者头梳双髻，红彩点染束发头绳；右立者披发无髻，发线两分；两人头发都用黑彩涂绘。右立者双臂张开，双掌竖起做鼓掌状。内着衰衣，外长袍，腰有束带，袍左衽大红色，绿领、绿边，黑轮廓线，彩色脱损，脖下戴串珠。左立者，右手攀前立者右肩头；左手搭于前立者左肩头，着衰衣，绿色长袍，左衽，腰有束带，红彩点束带领口，袍边黑色。就图像信息判断，此双人造型很可能是"和合"。"和合二仙"是有真人原型的。唐代宪宗时(806—821年)，浙江苏州"枫桥寒岩山"的庙内有两位僧人，一名寒山，一名拾得。寒山又名寒山子，据传是唐代贞观年间"应举不利，不群于俗，盖楚狂、沮溺之流"的一位诗僧，后隐居天台寒岩山。拾得是一个孤儿，被国清寺老僧丰于在天台山路过时发现并收养，故取名拾得(捡来的意思)。两僧自幼都有诗才，互相敬慕，遂成好友。天台山国清寺因而成为寒山、拾得的祖庭，内有他俩的画像，其文字描绘曰："寒山一印记，一手拊膝，微笑，赤足。拾得一手托珠，一手阅卷．亦赤足，大笑。"世人以此二人之和睦隐寓"和合"，取"和谐合好"，"以和为贵"，表达了人们向往真诚友爱的精神，所以后世称为，"和合二仙"。后人还辑有《寒山子集》留传于世。

9. Standing tomb-figure of He He

The 12-13th century
Height 27cm

The figurine is moulding and hollow, color of its figuline is lark, daubed the dressing-clay on its body, covered with transparent glaze, the bottom has an air-hole. The visual shape that is two men stand on the hexagonal pedestal, one lifted his arm on the other's shoulder, the pedestal is the shape of furniture, which was stippled red, green, and yellow colors, part of it was delineated black lines. The two men have delicate features, happy bearing. The left one combed double buns, the taenia which for binding the buns was stippled red color; the right one hasn't bun, hairstyle is a center parting; their hair were all painted with black color. The right one splayed his both arms out, erected his both hands like handclap, wears underclothing underneath, and wears long cope outside, loincloth around the waist, the cope that the front of the clothing is left, which has green collar, green border, black lines, the colors were faded, wears a string of beads on neck. The left one, who put his right hand on the other one's arm, and put the left hand over the other's left shoulder, wears underclothing and green long cope, the front of the clothing is left, loincloth around waist, the loincloth and collar was painted red color, border of the cope is black. From the image information, the two men should be "He He". "Two celestial beings He He" have the true mold. At the period of Xianzong Tang Dynasty (A.D.806-821), there have two monks in the temple of "Mount Hanyan of Maple Bridge" at Suzhou Zhejiang, one's name is Han Shan, the other one's name is Shi De. Han Shan alias Han Shanzi, it is said that he is a poem monk who "flunk in imperial examination, not comply with convention, like the men who are Chu Kuang (unruly man), Chang Ju and Jie Ni (all recluse)" at the period of Zhenguan Tang Dynasty, afterward, he lived be a hermit in Mount Tiantai Hanyan. Shi De is an orphan, found and adopted by an old monk of Guoqing Temple who is Feng Yu when he passes by Mount Tiantai, so named him Shi De (means picked). The two monks are all have the poetic talent from a child, adored each other, and then be friends. Thus the Mount Tiantai and the Guoqing Temple had become the home of Han Shan and Shi De, where have their figures on which there have words to describe that "Han Shan, one hand stroking knee, smiling, barefoot. Shi De, one hand lifting pearl, one hand holding book, also is barefoot, laughing." Earthling use the harmony of the two men to imply "He He", get the means "harmonious", "cherishing the value of harmony", expressed the spirit that people look forward to sincerity and friendship, they were called "Two celestial beings He He" by later generations. There had the HAN SHANZI ANTHOLOGY which collected by later generations bequeathed.

10、髡发抱匣俑

12—13世纪
高23.6厘米

　　胎色灰黄，模制中空，施化妆土，色白，通体罩透明釉，底部无釉露胎，有透气孔。造型为一年轻人抱匣立于方台上。年轻人发束双分，两缕头发垂于身前，黑彩涂绘，头顶髡剃，一圈无发，绿彩平涂显示髡剃后的绒发效果。此髡顶发饰为中原汉人所没有，北地辽契丹人、金女真人，及后世蒙元人多有此俗，髡发造型，在辽金元墓葬壁画及其他遗迹中常见。年轻人黑彩绘眉眼，红彩点唇，眉间额头有红彩点靥，身穿绿领裹袖左衽红袍，过膝，手包于袖中；红袍外罩白色碎花半臂，红线绿领边，碎花肩上四朵，有绿叶、背后一朵，全红；下着遮裙，前后两片，前片绿色下摆有黄色横边，中间品字形团花三朵，红圈白地上下两朵黄蕊红花，两侧绿点，后片全白；腰间遮裙上系三条带子，带子叠头三折；下身白裤黑鞋，鞋半露。右臂下垂，左臂屈弯，腋下夹一方匣子，匣子中绘三条黑线，一粗两细，成盖口效果，匣前面黄彩涂色，后面素白。脚下所站立方台为白色，有黑线涂框，前左右三面点涂黑弧圈成壶门效果，后面白色。河北省邯郸市峰峰矿区，泰和三年（1203年）"崔仙奴墓"中也出土有一件相类的抱匣俑，尺寸较小。从此俑的髡发及衣饰明显可确认其为异族或接受异族发式的中原人，最大可能就是金朝人。

10. Figurine of tonsure man with box

The 12-13th century
Height 23.6cm

　　The figurine is moulding and hollow, color of its figuline is lark, daubed the dressing-clay which color is white, covered with transparent glaze whole, the bottom which hasn't glaze and an air-hole on it. The visual shape that is a young man holds a box and stands on the quadrate pedestal. Hair of the young man has a center parting, two wisps of hair lolling on chest, was painted with black color, the calvaria was tonsured with no hair, and laid green color on it to express the effect of down. This tonsure hairstyle is not in the Hans, it is the habitude of Liao's Khitan, Jin's Nuchen, and Yuan's Mongol, this tonsure shape was frequently seen in the grave mural of Liao, Jin, and Yuan. The young man, who was painted eyebrows and eyes with black color, stippled lips with red color, stippled Ye (ornament on the cheek) on forehead with red color, wears red robe which came below knees, green collar, narrow sleeves, the front of the clothing is left, wrapped the hands in the sleeves; covers white Banbi (half sleeve) with flower patterns over the red robe, red line and green border, the flower patterns, four on the shoulder with green leaves, one on the back with all red color; wears cover-skirt which has two pieces the front and the back, the front piece which is green with yellow border at the lower hem, three cycloid flower patterns which have red ring in the form of Pin (Chinese character), and two red flowers with yellow pistil on the white background at the middle, the back piece is all white; the waist was tied three belts which tops folded three folds; wears white trousers, black shoes which were showed a half. The drooping right arm, bended left arm, under the armpit there has an oblong box which was painted three black lines to get the effect of cover's rim, one is thick but two are thin, painted yellow color front of the box, the back is white. The quadrate pedestal is white with black frame, the front, left and right sides were painted black arc-shaped like Kunmen, the back is white. The Feng Feng mining area of Handan, Hebei province, at where it has the "Cui Xiannu Tomb" which in the third year of Taihe (A.D. 1203) period, unearthed an analogous figurine, lesser size. The figurine, from the decorations that the cloth and the tonsure, it can be affirm that the man is different race or the Han who accepted the hairstyle of different race, the most probably that he should be the Jin people.

11、白衣交手文吏像

12-13世纪
高27.8厘米

　　胎色灰黄较酥松，模制中空，施化妆土，罩透明釉，多处露胎，器底有透气孔。造型为一交手文吏坐于石台之上。文吏头戴软脚幞头，黑彩涂绘，幞头脚垂于两肩。黑彩绘眉眼，大鼻，红彩点唇，面颊用粉色晕染，鼻翼下两撇黑胡过唇角，下巴颏处一缕长髯近胸，两鬓也有两缕垂髯。身着左衽窄袖白花袍，领口、衣边、袖口都是绿色；上身肩、腹部，有三朵倒品字形黄彩红边云头纹饰；下身两腿膝盖及腿间有横排黄彩红边云头纹饰；腰系黑色丝绦，两个带头有垂穗。文吏双手交叉握举胸前，红彩绘手指轮廓，粉色晕染表现肤色，脚蹬黑鞋，袍遮盖半露；身下所坐石台，黑彩半涂。同类型白衣文吏的标本，北京故宫博物院有藏。

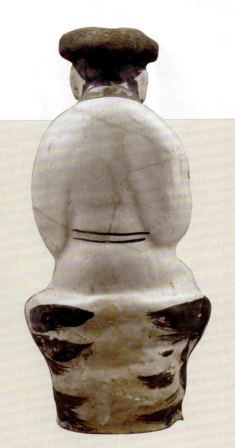

11. White cloth civilian who cups one hand in the other figurine

The 12-13th century
Height 27.8cm

　　The figurine is moulding and hollow, its figuline is lark and loose, daubed the dressing-clay on its body, and covered with transparent glaze, bared the roughcast many place, and an air-hole on the bottom. The visual shape that is a civilian who cups one hand in the other sits on the stone platform. The civilian wares Putou (one of a cap in antiquity) with soft-horns, painted with black color, the horns of Putou lolling to the shoulders. The eyebrows and eyes were painted with black color, big nose, stippled lips with red color, the cheeks was dyed incarnadine, black splay-beard under the nose, the chin at where it has a wisp of long whiskers close to chest, and the two temples also have two wisps of whiskers. Wears white robe which has flower patterns, the collar, border, and cuffs are all green, the front of the cloth is left; three cloud-shape patterns which are yellow color with red edge on the shoulders and belly in the form of inverse Pin (Chinese character); three same patterns on the two knees and between of the knees in the horizontal; ties black silk-ribbon which has two ends with tassels around waist. The civilian, who cups one hand in the other before the chest, the contours of fingers were painted with red color, dyed incarnadine; wears black shoes which were showed a half on feet; the stone platform which was sat by this civilian was painted half with black color. The same stamp of the civilian figurine was collected by The Palace Museum Beijing.

12、白衣文吏像

12—13世纪
高22厘米

　　胎色灰黄，模制中空，施化妆土，罩透明釉，色白，器底有透气孔。造型为一文吏坐于圆凳之上。文吏头戴硬幞头，黑彩涂绘，两侧有孔，疑其当时可以插硬脚。黑彩绘眉眼，红彩点唇，面颊用粉色晕染，鼻翼下两撇黑胡过唇角，下巴颏处一缕长髯近胸，两鬓也有两缕垂髯。衷衣红色黄领，外罩广袖圆领白花袍，领口绿色红边，袖口黑色衬绿红边；白袍两边袖上及肩部各有三朵碎花，胸前一朵，下身正面品字形三朵，碎花红绿黄彩点绘。腰系红带，后腰能看到，带板五块。文吏右手跷指持物，似书卷；左手垂于膝上，红彩绘手指轮廓，粉色晕染表现肤色；脚蹬黑鞋，袍遮盖半露。身下所坐圆凳底部黑线绿框。从整体人物形制看，模制白样有清晰的衣褶及器座轮廓线，这种轮廓线的处理，给彩绘带来了更准确的指示。

12. White cloth civilian figurine

The 12-13th century
Height 22cm

　　The figurine is moulding and hollow, lark figuline, daubed the dressing-clay on its body, and covered with transparent glaze, color is white, and an air-hole on the bottom. The visual shape that is a civilian sits on a roundness stool. The civilian wears a hard Putou on head, painted with black color, the two sides have holes which maybe the place to insert the hard-horns. The eyebrows and eyes were painted with black color, stippled lips with red color, the cheeks was dyed incarnadine, black splay-beard under the nose, the chin at where it has a wisp of long whiskers close to chest, and the two temples also have two wisps of whiskers. Wears underclothing which is red with yellow collar, on which covers white robe with flower patterns, wide sleeves, the collar is green with red line; the cuffs, which has black lining and green border with red line; the white robe, each sleeve has three flower-patterns, one flower-pattern on the chest, three flower-patterns below that in the form of Pin, those flower-patterns were painted with red, green, and yellow colors. Ties red girdle around the waist, from the back of waist it can be seen five pieces of plate. The civilian hold something like a volume in his right hand and holds up the little finger; puts the left hand on the knee, the contours of fingers were painted with red color, dyed incarnadine; wears black shoes which were showed a half on feet. The roundness stool has black and green lines, which was sat by this civilian. From the whole shape and structure, it can be seen that the moulding has clear-cut lines of pleats and stool's contour line, that brought more exact guide for painted colors.

13、文士立俑

12—13世纪
高21厘米

胎色灰黄酥松，模制中空，施化妆土，罩透明釉，器底有透气孔。文吏立于方台上。文吏黑发披肩，一条巾带（似为红彩脱色）束发，分垂两边。黑彩绘眉眼，鼻翼下两撇黑胡过唇角，下巴颏处一缕长髯，两鬓有两缕垂髯。身着藤黄色半臂披肩，腰系绦带。文士面向右侧转，右手握拳举于胸前，左手下垂，手腕有饰物。模制身体有多层轮廓，神态生动。可惜俑身多锈蚀剥损，釉彩保存状况不好。

13. Standing tomb-figure of man

The 12-13th century
Height 21cm

The figurine is moulding and hollow, its figuline is lark and loose, daubed the dressing-clay on its body, covered with transparent glaze, and an air-hole on the bottom. A man whose hair falls to his shoulders stands on the square platform, there has a band (the color maybe red) worn around his head and hung on each shoulder. The eyebrows and eyes were painted with black color, black splay-beard under the nose, the chin at where it has a wisp of long whiskers, and the two temples also have two wisps of whiskers. He wears gamboges half-sleeve fanon, ties silk-ribbon around waist. This man faced to the right side, the right hand made a fist before chest, the left hand hung, there have accouterment on hands. The moulding body has several layers of contour, bearing is vivid. It's regretted that it was eroded much, the glaze-color which was saved badly.

14、方尖帽骑马偶

12—13世纪
高14.5厘米，纵长9.8厘米

灰胎，质坚，模制，施化妆土，色白，外
罩玻璃釉，玻化程度高。骑者戴四角尖帽，帽
顶画黑线点黄彩，腭下脖子处有黑色帽带系扎，
身着绿色黑花长袍，鞋黑色，马镫白色。黑彩绘
眉眼，唇无点色。身下白马，马鞍黄彩涂抹，马鬃
是模印出来的，缰索用黑彩勾绘。就器物观察，黑彩为釉
下。人物骑乘马上，身微前倾，左手揽缰，右手握拳，头左顾
做沉思状。全器仅黄、绿彩，有土蚀，未见红彩。此类不施红
彩之器少见，有"素三彩"的韵味。人物所戴四方尖角帽，典
型胡样，非中原汉地之俗。这种帽式在边疆地区及金元考古
材料中多见。

14. Figurine of equestrian with spire square-hat

The 12-13th century
Height 14.5cm, longitudinal length 9.8cm

The roughcast, which is grey, flinty quality, moulding,
daubed the dressing-clay which color is white, on which it
was covered with vitreous glaze, the degree of vitrification
is higher. Equestrian wears foursquare spire hat which was
painted black color and stippled yellow color on the top, ties
black hat-band under the neck, wears green long robe with
black patterns, shoes are black, and stirrups are white. The
eyebrows and eyes was painted with black color, lips has
no color. White horse, the saddle was laid on yellow color,
horse mane was stamped, halter was delineated with black
color. This ware, the black color is under glaze. One man
rode on the horse, whose body leaning forward, left hand
holding the halter, right hand made a fist, face to left side
to be meditator. The whole ware only has yellow and green
colors which were corroded by earth, but no red color. This
kind of ware which hasn't red color has been seldom seen, it
has the aroma of "plain tricolor". The foursquare spire hat
is the typical Hu-style, not the Han-style. This style of hat
has been often seen in border area and the archaeological
materials of Jin and Yuan dynasties.

15、方幞头持莲俑

12—13世纪
高12厘米

胎色灰黄，模制中空，施化妆土，罩透明釉，底有透气孔。造型为一小童持莲蹲坐，头戴方幞头，黑彩涂绘，中起凸有轮廓线。黑彩绘眉眼，红彩点唇，面颊用粉色晕染，眼角有点靥。上身内衷衣左衽红边黄色，外罩白地红绿色团花短袄；两肩袖各有两朵团花，背心一朵；团花外红圈内绿圈中心两点红。下身着红色遮裙，胸腰部绿色束带；裤白色，点红点花。小童左手上，右手下，向右侧倒持绿叶红莲花斜置，神态俏皮。就此俑尺寸和题材，应该属于当时的儿童玩具。

15. Figurine of child who wears square Putou holds lotus

The 12-13th century
Height 12cm

The figurine is moulding and hollow, lark figuline, daubed the dressing-clay on its body, and covered with transparent glaze, an air-hole on the bottom. The visual shape that is a squat child holds lotus, wears square Putou which was painted with black color, middle of it is raised. The eyebrows and eyes were painted with black color, stippled lips with red color, the cheeks was dyed incarnadine, sides of the eyes were stippled Ye (ornament on the cheek). Wears yellow underclothing which with red border, the front of cloth is left, covers short coat which has green and red flower patterns on the white background outer; two round patterns on each shoulder, and one on the middle of back; the round patterns which have red and green rings and two red spots in the middle. Wears red cover-skirt, ties green band at the chest; the trousers is white, stippled red patterns. The child's left hand up, right hand down, holds a branch of lotus inversely, nifty manner. The size and the subject of figurine, it should be the toy for children to play at that time.

16、童子读书坐俑

12—13世纪
横宽12.8厘米，高12.6厘米

　　胎色灰黄，质酥松，模制中空，施化妆土，罩透明釉，器底有透气孔。造型是一童子持书侧靠卧休憩。童子圆头大耳，黑彩绘眉眼，红彩点唇，眼微眯，神色清秀。脖颈戴如意云头样黄色项饰（似意为黄金制）。内穿红色黑线绿领无袖短褂，露胸及胳膊；腹部淡绿色红黄圈花包肚，胸及腹部有带子打花结；外罩绿色黑点花束袖衫，黑点花四点一组，敞怀，领口下翻，挂于背心及前臂处，袖口黑彩勾"回纹"，涂黄釉。下身着红色黄点花裤，点花是中间一个大的外缘一圈十多个小点；腿盘交，露一只黑鞋。童子右臂屈支，身后倚，手拳握，肘臂、肋部压一黑框涂黄彩绿面方座；左臂垂伸，左手持一本翻开书册，搭在左膝上，书册上有黑彩画写。书角破损，破损处以绿彩点涂，似烤花前的旧伤，为加彩烤花时刻意遮盖。就此童子像衣服及露臂形态，基本可推测，所描绘的是夏日午后读书休憩的一幕，外衣多衣线纹路及点花，突出的是纱丝清凉织物的意境，深具写实效果。

16. Sitting tomb-figure of child reading book

The 12-13th century
Width 12.8cm, height 12.6cm

　　The figurine is moulding and hollow, its figuline is lark and loose, daubed the dressing-clay on its body, covered with transparent glaze, and an air-hole on the bottom. The visual shape is a child who holds a book and lies on his side to rest. The child, round head, big ears, the eyebrows and eyes were painted with black color, the lips were stippled with red color, narrowed his eyes, comeliness look. The child wears sautoir which is Ruyi-cloud shape and yellow color (means gold) on neck. Red short Gua (a Chinese-style jacket) which has green collar, black lines, and no sleeves, which was worn inner, the chest and arms are all bare; wears pea green Baodu (a band for wrap belly) which has yellow and red patterns, ties a knot under the chest; the green narrow-sleeve clothing with black patterns which are groups of four spots, that was worn outer, the front of this clothing is open, the turndown neckline hung at the back and arms, the cuffs was drawn "Huiwen (fret, design consisting of repeated figures)" with black color, laid yellow glaze on. He wears red trousers with yellow flower-patterns which shape are a big spot in the middle with multispot outer; crossed his legs, showed one black shoe. The child, bent his right arm to underprop, leaning his body backwards against a square yellow seat which has black frame and green surface, made the right hand a fist; the left hand which holds one open book on his left knee. The open book which was drawn the black lines, the corner dilapidated, the breakage was daubed with green color, as if damaged before decorating fire, it was covered designedly. The cloth and the bare arms of this child, these characteristic showed an act that had a rest after read book in the afternoon of summer, the outer wear has more lines and spots patterns, that to lay stress on the pleasantly cool felling from the voile silk fabric, it has the true-life effect deeply.

17、襁褓俑

13世纪
高4.6厘米   长18.3厘米   宽6.5厘米

　　灰黄色胎，模制，施化妆土，罩透明釉，背后无釉露胎，上半身釉水明亮，下半身有涩感，在婴儿的臀部扎有透气孔。头顶剔发留鬃，涂绿彩表示剔发以后的头皮，短绒眉，小眼红唇，大囟门，重下巴，面颊粉红色晕染，眉顶额间有两个红月、一个红圆圈点绿的"花钿"。身着绿领红色绿花"半臂"短襦，内衣对开红领，颈部有项饰。右手拳举，左手垂下，戴金（黄彩）手镯，仰卧，从胸腰以下至膝头由四道绿、红绿、红相间的系带捆扎。此样式襁褓俑，1985年5月，河北省邯郸市峰峰矿区"崔仙奴墓"（见：秦大树、李喜仁、马忠理《邯郸市峰峰矿区出土的两批红绿彩瓷器》，《文物》1997年　第10期，P30页和彩色插页贰1)有出土，海外也有收藏（HE LI：《CHINESE CERAMICS--THE NEW STANDARD GUIDE》1996 The Asian Art museum Of san Francisco. THAMES AND HUDSON. Picture 323）。

17. The swaddled baby figurine

The 13th century
Height 4.6cm, Length 18.3cm, Width 6.5cm

　　The figuline is lark, moulding, daubed the body with dressing-clay, and then covered transparent glaze, bare back without glaze. The glaze of the upper part of the body is brightness, glaze of the lower part of the body is dull, it was poked an air hole on the baby's buttocks. Shaved hair but left Jiu (hair bun) on the top of the head, the bare scalp was painted with green color, short eyebrows, little eyes, vermilion lips, big fontanel, double chins, the cheek was dyed be carnation, there have "Hua Dian (one of ornament like flower) over eyebrows, two red crescent moon, one red circle in which was stippled green color. Wears "Ban Bi (half sleeves)" short jacket which is green collar, red background, and green flowers, undergarment has red collar, sautoir on the neck. Fists right hand, hangs the left hand, wares gold (yellow color) bracelet, lies on his back, from the waist to the knees, there have four ribbons which are green, red, green, and red color. This style of the swaddled baby figurine, which had been unearthed from the "Tomb of Cui Xiannu" (see: Qin Dashu, Li Xiren and Ma Zongli, "TWO GROUPS OF RED AND GREEN PORCELAINS UNEARTHED AT FENGFENG MINING AREA HANDAN", WENWU, 10, 1997, P30 and chromatic inset 2-1) of Fengfeng diggings Handan Hebei Province, it was collected by overseas (He Li, CHINESE CERAMICS--THE NEW STANDARD GUIDE, 1996, The Asian Art Museum Of San Francisco, THAMES AND HUDSON, Picture 323) too.

18、童子坐鼓凳抱琴俑

12—13世纪
高15.8厘米

　　灰黑色胎，模制，施化妆土，罩玻璃釉，多细碎开片，仅圈足露胎，底部扎有透气孔。黑彩绘眉、眼、发，发饰为"鹁角"，剔发处用淡绿彩涂抹显示头皮绒发的效果，红色涂唇，身着圆领衣，肩部从左至右披扎绿色红花锦带，右手持带，左手抱琴，骑坐在由黑彩装饰的鼓凳上，鼓凳有模印花，底有气孔，气孔旁黑彩釉下书款"李家造"，在已知红绿彩瓷塑中，有书款记者甚少。此俑最特殊的就是"琴"的出现。"琴"，在古代又称"瑶琴"，现代称古琴、七弦琴，它是中国历代文人雅士所崇尚的乐器之一。在中国古代文献如《诗经》、《左传》、《国语》、《吕氏春秋》等都有记载。此童子俑所抱的"琴"，以写实手法处理，外框黄彩，代替黄色髹漆，琴首为如意云式，岳山也做云头式，涂绿彩，额为菱方形，中间绷琴弦九根。宋朝徽宗赵佶就非常热爱琴艺，曾广罗尽搜天下名琴藏于特设之"万琴堂"中。因此在这件12—13世纪的童子俑中出现古琴，也恰反映了，当时社会的一种艺术风尚。

18. The child holds Qin in arms and sits on drum figurine

The 12-13th century
Height 15.8cm

The figuline is grey black, moulding, daubed dressing-clay on the body, and then covered the transparent glaze, on which it has many finely-broken clastic grains, only the circled foot of the figurine is bare, on which it was poked an air hole. The eyebrows, eyes, and hair were painted with black color, the hairstyle is "Bo Jiao (one of the child's hairstyle", applied viridescent color on the tonsure expressed the down, spread the lips red, wears round-neck clothing, drapes brocade ribbon which is green background red flower pattern over left shoulder, the right hand holds ribbon, but holds Qin in his left arm, rids on black drum which was stamped flower pattern, the bottom has an air hole, side of the hole on where has the Chinese characters "Li Jia Zao" which were written with black color under-glaze, it is rare that which has the mark of Chinese characters in the known red and green porcelain-figurine. The most especial of this figurine is appearance of the "Qin". "Qin", it was called "Yao Qin (peptachord)" in antiquity, but in modern times it is called ancient Qin or seven-stringed instrument, it is among the musical instruments which were advocated by brahmin in past dynasties of China, and it was recorded in the Chinese ancient literatures such as SHI JING (THE BOOK OF SONGS), ZUO ZHUAN, GUO YU, LV SHI CHUN QIU (THE SPRING AND AUTUMN ANNALS OF LV). The "Qin" that was held by the child in his arm, its facture is true-life, the outline border used yellow color as a substitute for lacquer, the head of the Qin is Ruyi-shape, Yue Shan (parts of Qin, a stretcher to prop the strings) also is Ruyi-shape, and smeared green color on it, E (parts of Qin) is rhombus, nine strings. Zhao Ji the emperor of Song Dynasty who had deep love on art of Qin, gathered the rare Qin from all over the world and collected them in "Wan Qin Tang (stores of myriad Qin)". Thus this ancient Qin that appeared on the child figurine of the 12-13th century reflects an artistic fashion of the society at that time.

19、骑鼓执莲童子偶

12—13世纪
高17.5厘米

灰胎，施化妆土，罩透明釉，模制中空，器底有透气孔。黑彩绘眉、眼、发、衣纹、鞋尖及鼓的轮廓，孩童发饰为"鹁角"，剃发处用很淡的绿彩涂抹显示头皮绒发的效果。唇点红彩，脸颊、脖子及手外露部用粉红色渲染表示肤色。上身着白色圆领衫，领口、袖口有红黄色，下身着绿裙系红带，白裤有红绿边，黑鞋，肩披红色点黄点的帛带，手中执绿色莲叶坐于圆鼓上，双腿下垂，鼓线黑彩勾绘。1974年禹县扒村瓷窑遗址采集到一件执莲童子俑和此相近。这类形制的玩偶，同宋金时"七夕（乞巧）节"的摩睺罗有关系，当时多在市肆售卖，《东京梦华录》中有载。

19. Figurine of child holds lotus-leaf rides on drum

The 12-13th century
Height 17.5cm

The roughcast, which is grey, was daubed the dressing-clay and covered transparent glaze, it is moulding and hollow, the bottom has an air-hole. The eyebrows, eyes, hair, cloth patterns, toecaps, and the outline of drum are all black color, this child's hairstyle is "Bojiao (one of the child's hairstyle in China)", and applied viridescent color on the tonsure expressed the down. Lips were stippled red color, the face, neck, hands, and all bare skin were dyed with nude pink to show the color of skin. Wears white cloth with circinal collar, the neckline and cuffs have red and yellow colors; wears green skirt and ties red broad belt, white trousers with red and green border, black shoes, drapes silk belt which is red with yellow spots over his shoulder, holds green lotus-leaf in hands, sits on the round drum which was drawn black lines. In 1974, a figurine of child holds lotus which same as this one, was collected in kiln site of Pacun, Yuxian. This kind of toy figurine, has the connection with Mohouluo (Sanskrit is Mahoraga) of "Qixi (the 7th evening of the 7th) or Qiqiao (begging for a cleverness ceremony) festival" at the period of Song and Jin dynasties, it was sold in downtown streets at that time, that was recorded by DONG JING MENG HUA LU (RECOLLECT THE FLOURISHING DONGJING.).

20、童子执莲坐偶

12—13世纪
高17.3厘米

胎色灰黄，质酥松，模制中空，施化妆土，罩透明釉，器底有透气孔。造型是一童子持荷叶莲花坐于鼓凳上。童子黑彩绘眉眼，红彩点唇，发饰为"鹁角"，有四个抓鬏，红色系绳。脖颈戴宽箍锁形红边黄色项饰（似意为黄金）。身穿红黄色圈花绿半臂，圈花外红内涂黄色中心点红点，左右肩各一朵，背后四朵；领口黑蔓草花边，敞怀，胸部半露；腹部黄色包肚，近胸处有带子打花结；手腕处有黄色手镯。下穿红裤，黑鞋。左腿屈搭于鼓凳上，右腿下垂。左手握莲梗微上举于胸部，右手拿荷叶莲花置于右膝上。身下所坐鼓凳黑色，近足处内收，有黄色如意形开光券门，内绿色；凳面白色。从背后可以发现，孩童红裤开裆，露腚。此偶同前述"骑鼓执莲童子偶"造型相近。

20. Sitting tomb-figure of child holds lotus-leaf

The 12-13th century
Height 17.3cm

The figurine is moulding and hollow, its figuline is lark and loose, daubed the dressing-clay on its body, covered with transparent glaze, and an air-hole on the bottom. The visual shape is a child who holds the lotus-leaf sits on the drum-stool. It was painted the eyebrows and eyes with black color, stippled the lips with red color, the hairstyle is "Bojiao", four hair-buns which were ties with red taenia. The child wears yellow color (means gold) sautoir which is wide and lock-shape with red edge on the neck. Wears the green Banbi (half-sleeve cloth) with red and yellow color patterns which shaped like a ball, that were painted red outline, color in yellow, and stippled red dots in the middle, two patterns on each shoulder, four on the back; the neckline has black tendril patterns purfle, the front of this clothing is open; wears yellow Baodu (a band for wrap belly), and ties a knot under the chest; wears yellow bracelets at both wrists. Red trousers and black shoes. The left leg bent on the drum-stool, the right leg hang. The left hand holds in the peduncle at the chest, the right hand holds the lotus on the right knee. The black drum-stool, which has inward concave close to the foot, on which has the pattern that is yellow Ruyi-shape arch-door, with green color inside; surface of the drum-stool is white. Look at it from the its back, the crotch of child's red trousers is opening bare the buttocks. This tomb-figure is similar to foregoing "Figurine of child holds lotus-leaf rides on drum".

21、童子玩雀偶

12—13世纪
高15.8厘米

　　胎色灰黄，模制中空，施化妆土，罩透明釉，器底有透气孔。造型是一孩童站立玩雀。发式双分，头顶有剃发，剃发处用淡绿彩涂抹显示头皮绒发的效果。黑彩绘眉眼，红彩点唇，面颊用粉色晕染；鼻梁和面颊黑彩画丑，完全是摹仿宋金丑戏装扮，此装扮，宋金壁画、砖刻及陶瓷制品中多见。王国维《古剧脚色考》中对"丑"有较详描述。孩童身着绿色黑花半长衫，敞怀露胸腹，领口红色，内领口淡绿色外翻，衣褶线黑彩勾绘，前后两片开衩，腰有系绳，穿红裤，腰下半接黄色；足蹬黑鞋。右手抓雀，置于右胸口，雀黄色黑彩绘羽，左手放腰部，攥绳，绳拴雀腿。童子两腿微分跨，左腿前，右腿后，胯间有一黑彩黄色雀笼，笼顶圆形红衬，上有提环，整个造型呈锥状，横竖木竹条编就，笼口处卧一欲飞黄雀。此偶类同前述，应该也是宋金时的摩睺罗玩具。

21. Tomb-figure of child plays sparrow

The 12-13th century
Height 15.8cm

　　The figurine is moulding and hollow, its figuline is lark, daubed the dressing-clay on its body, covered with transparent glaze, and an air-hole on the bottom. The visual shape is a standing child who is playing the sparrow. He's hair divides to either side, top of the head was shaven a circle, and applied viridescent color on the tonsure expressed the down. The eyebrows and eyes were painted with black color, stippled lips with red color, the cheeks was dyed incarnadine; on the cheeks and bridge of nose it was painted Chou (face-paint of zany), it take example by the zany's toilette of Song and Jin dynasties, this toilette that had been seen much in the mural, carved brick, and the ceramics of Song and Jin dynasties. It has more detailed description for "Chou (zany)" in GU JU JIAO SE KAO (ROLE IN ANACIENT OPERAS) by Wang guowei. The child wears green midi with black patterns, the front of this cloth is open, bare belly and chest, red collar, the pea green inner collar was turned outward, the line of cloth's pleats were drawn by black color, slits at the sides of midi, ties belt around waist; red trousers with yellow color upside; wears black shoes on feet. The child clutched the sparrow which has yellow and black feathers to her breast with right hand; the left hand grasped the rope which tied the sparrow's leg at waist. The child is standing, left leg forward, right leg backward, and between legs where has a yellow birdcage with black lines, the birdcage, which has red vault with ring-tab, the whole shape like a taper, it was woven by interlacing sawali, a sparrow who itch to fly in the gate. This tomb-figure is similar to the foregoing one, should be the Mahoraga toy either in Song and Jin times.

22—1、童子执莲叶偶

12—13世纪
高18厘米

　　胎色深灰，模制中空，施化妆土，多处露胎，罩透明釉不到底，器底有透气孔。造型是一童子持荷叶坐于鼓凳上。童子黑彩绘眉眼，红彩点唇，发饰为"鹁角"，有四个抓髻，红色系绳。身着红色半长衫，绿领，前身藤黄色点碎花，勾绘腰间系带，背后无花，全红，前后两片开衩；内衷衣红色点黄领；下身绿裤勾红边，鞋白色。所坐鼓凳白色，有黑彩勾如意形开光券门，身后未遮盖处，能看到鼓凳上沿的模印鼓钉轮廓；右腿屈蹬鼓凳膝上举，左腿下垂。左右手屈置胸前，左手中有绿色拳卷荷叶，黑彩勾叶脉。

22-1. Tomb-figure of child holds lotus-leaf

The 12-13th century
Height 18cm

　　The figurine is moulding and hollow, its figuline is dark gray, daubed the dressing-clay on its body, bared the roughcast many place, covered with transparent glaze without the bottom on which has an air-hole. The visual shape that is a child holds the lotus-leaf sits on the drum-stool. It was painted the eyebrows and eyes with black color, stippled the lips with red color, the hairstyle is "Bojiao", four hair-buns which were ties with red taenia. The child wears red midi with green collar, stippled the gamboge small flower-patterns on the front, drawn a belt at the waist, the back is red without patterns, slits at the sides; the underclothing has yellow collar which with spots pattern; green trousers with red border, white shoes. The white drum-stool, was drawn a Xuanmen (arch door) which is Ruyi-shape, see it's back which hasn't the cover, it has the drum-pegs border which are stamped on the upside; the child, bent his right leg stepped on the drum-stool, hang his left leg. Both hands before the chest, the left hand holds the green curly lotus-leaf which was drawn the nervation by black color.

22—2、童子执傀儡偶

12—13世纪
高17.8厘米

　　胎色深灰，模制中空，施化妆土，多处露胎，罩透明釉不到底，器底有透气孔。造型是一童子持傀儡坐于鼓凳上。童子黑彩绘眉眼，红彩点唇，发饰为"鹁角"，有四个抓髻，红色系绳。身着红色左衽半长衫，绿领，前身藤黄色点碎花，勾绘腰间系带，背后无花，全红，前后两片开衩；内衷衣红色点黄领；下身绿裤勾红边，鞋白色。所坐鼓凳白色，有黑彩勾如意形开光券门，身后未遮盖处，能看到鼓凳上沿的模印鼓钉轮廓；双腿分列下垂。左右手握于胸前，持一绿色带棒傀儡；傀儡黑彩勾绘，有帽，唇点红。就形制，可确认童子手持是典型的"杖头傀儡"。关于傀儡戏，周密《武林旧事》卷六"诸色伎艺人"有记，孟元老《东京梦华录》亦有载。

　　这两件持莲及傀儡的童子偶尺寸几乎完全相同，相貌、衣饰、色彩、绘画技法都一致。仅是腿的摆放形式和手中持物有差异，可以确认这是成对一组的玩具。

22-2. Tomb-figure of child holds the puppet

The 12-13th century
Height 17.8cm

　　The figurine is moulding and hollow, its figuline is dark gray, daubed the dressing-clay on its body, bared the roughcast many place, covered with transparent glaze without the bottom on which has an air-hole. The visual shape that is a child holds the puppet sits on the drum-stool. It was painted the eyebrows and eyes with black color, stippled the lips with red color, the hairstyle is "Bojiao", four hair-buns which were ties with red taenia. The child wears red midi with green collar, stippled the gamboge small flower-patterns on the front, drawn a belt at the waist, the back is red without patterns, slits at the sides; the underclothing has yellow collar which with spots pattern; green trousers with red border, white shoes. The white drum-stool, was drawn a Xuanmen (arch door) which is Ruyi-shape, see it's back which hasn't the cover, it has the drum-pegs border which are stamped on the upside; hang the legs at each side. This child, clasps the both hands before chest, and holds one green puppet which with stick; the puppet which has a hat, that was painted with black color, lips were stippled red. The puppet can be affirmed that it is the typical "puppet manipulated by sticks" from its shape and structure. About the puppet play, it has recorded by "The Different Performer" which in vol.6 of WU LIN JIU SHI (THE PAST THINGS ABOUT WULIN) by Zhou Mi, and the DONG JING MENG HUA LU (RECOLLECT THE FLOURISHING DONGJING.) which written by Meng Yuanlao also has the records.

　　These two tomb-figures have the uniform size almost, the appearances, costumes, colors, and technique of painting are all identical. Only have the two differences which are the legs' form and the things held in hand, it can be affirmed that they are the twin toys.

23-1、乐人立俑

12—13世纪
高18厘米

胎色灰黄，模制中空，施化妆土，色白，罩透明釉，器底有透气孔。年青人弹奏站立像，黑彩绘眉眼，红彩点唇，头戴黑色包巾有两个软脚。内穿黄色衷衣绿领；外罩红色藤黄花襦，绿领，花都在前身，后背全红；下身着红裤，外罩绿裙，脚穿白靴。裙有模印轮廓，后身无色；两条束带，前有搭片，红色包黄边，当为弹奏垫衬，放乐器附件之用。乐器斜横置，年青人左手半举捏龙首，右手弹拨，音箱倭方形；从龙首处可辨认绷弦两根。此两弦乐器，名"二弦琵琶"，也称其为"忽雷"，但倭方形者少见，20世纪30年代，上海大同乐会，仿制过的忽雷就是倭方形，样子更像三弦。

23-1. Standing tomb-figure of the player

The 12-13th century
Height 18cm

The figurine is moulding and hollow, its figuline is lark, daubed the dressing-clay on its body, color is white, and covered with transparent glaze, the bottom has an air-hole. The standing figurine that is a young man plays the musical instruments, black eyebrows and eyes, red lips, wears black scarf which has two soft-horns on head. The young man, who wears yellow underclothing with green collar; wears red Ru (short coat) which has gamboge flowers on the front, green collarband, red back; wears red trousers, covered green skirt outside, wears white boots. The skirt was stamped the figure, back of the skirt is white; two bands at the waist, it has a little piece of cloth which is red with the yellow border at the front, which should be the pad for the musical instrument to put some appurtenances inside. The musical instrument was set diagonal, its head was held by the young man's left hand, his right hand plucked it, the sound-box is quadrate with the roundish-angle; it can be found two chords from the pattern of musical instrument's head. This musical instrument with two chords, which was named "dwochord", also was called "Hulei", but saw little of it which shape is quadrate with roundish-angle, in 1930', the Shanghai Datong Music Union had copied one Hulei which shape is quadrate with roundish-angle, its appearance is more like trichord.

23-2、乐人立俑

12—13世纪
高19厘米

　　胎色灰黄，模制中空，施化妆土，色白，罩透明釉，器底有透气孔。年青人弹奏站立像，黑彩绘眉眼，红彩点唇，头戴黑色包巾有两个软脚。内穿衷衣绿领；外罩红色绿花襦，黄领，后背红线勾轮廓，无花；下身着红线白裤，外罩红圈绿花白裙，脚穿白靴。裙有模印轮廓，后身红线勾轮廓，无花；腰部两条束带，前有搭片，绿地红圈花包黄边，弹奏垫衬。乐器斜横置，年青人左手半举捏龙首，右手弹拨，音箱梨圆形；黄杆红边。此俑和前弹倭方忽雷立俑的人物姿势相同，仅是所持乐器方圆有差异。这类乐器，称为"忽雷"，刘世珩《双忽雷本事·小忽雷记》载："忽雷即鳄鱼，其齿骨作乐器有异响"。《文献通考》还是将其归入琵琶类。

23-2. Standing tomb-figure of the player

The 12-13th century
Height 19cm

　　The figurine is moulding and hollow, its figuline is lark, daubed the dressing-clay on its body, color is white, and covered with transparent glaze, the bottom has an air-hole. The standing figurine that is a young man plays the musical instruments, black eyebrows and eyes, red lips, wears black scarf which has two soft-horns on head. The young man, who wears underclothing with green collar; wears red Ru (short coat) with flowers pattern, yellow collar, the back was drawn the red lines without flowers; white trousers with red lines, covered white skirt which has the patterns of red circle and green flower outside, wears white boots on the feet. The skirt was stamped the figure, the back was drawn the red lines without flowers; two bands at the waist, it has a little piece of cloth which has red circle flower-patterns on the green background and with the yellow border at the front, that is the pad for the musical instrument. The musical instrument was set diagonal, its head was held by the young man's left hand, his right hand plucked it, the sound-box is pyriform; yellow staff and red border. The posture of this tomb-figure is same as foregoing the standing tomb-figure of plays the quadrate Hulei, only have the different about the musical instrument's shape. This kind of musical instrument was called "Hulei", the SHUANG HU LEI BEN SHI ·XIAO HU LEI JI by Liu shihang, that recorded "Hulei is the crocodile, use its teeth and bones to make the musical instrument which will have preternatural sound". Hulei, it was ranged to lute species by WEN XIAN TONG KAO (LITERATURE ENCYCLOPEDIA).

24-1、抱瓶俑（红衣）

12-13世纪
高15.8厘米

胎色灰黄，质酥松，模制中空，施化妆土，罩透明釉，底无孔。造型是一仆俑抱瓶跪坐，发束双分，两缕头发垂于身前，黑彩涂绘，头顶髡剃，一圈无发，绿彩平涂显示髡剃后的绒发效果。黑彩绘眉眼，身穿束袖绿领点藤黄花红袍，掩襟。腰系绿革带，背后束扎；带左边悬挂竖囊包（可能是盛放刀筷用具的），黑彩绘涂黄色；带右挂荷包，圆形，黑色涂黄彩。左手环屈，右手托抱梅瓶；瓶身黑色口白圈，近口处有黄箍圈；瓶口有孔中空，巧妙的达到俑像烧造透气的效果。双腿跪地，臀压坐脚后跟上。从衣饰、抱瓶和跪坐姿态，可以判断其属于仆俑。仆俑所抱的黑瓶，在金元时期的墓葬中多有出土，属于酒瓶。

24-1. Tomb-figure of man holds bottle (red cloth)

The 12-13th century
Height 15.8cm

The figurine is moulding and hollow, its figuline is lark and loose, daubed the dressing-clay on its body, covered with transparent glaze, the bottom without air-hole. The visual shape which is a servant holds a bottle in his arm and kneels. He's hair divides to either side, two wisps of hair which was painted by black color lolling on the front of body, the calvaria was tonsured with no hair, and laid green color on it to express the effect of down. The child whose eyebrows and eyes was painted with black color, wears red robe which has narrow-sleeves, green collar, gamboge flower-patterns, the covered garment's front. Ties green hide-band around waist, the back has the knot; at the left side of the waist where was tied a long black bag (maybe to set the knife and the chopsticks) which painted with yellow color; at the right side of the waist where was tied black pouch which is nummular, drawn the yellow color. The left arm bent, the right hand held a mei-bottle; the bottle is black with white brim, it has a yellow hoop near the rim; the bottle is hollow, and on its mouth where has a hole to be the airflow orifice for the tomb-figure ingenious. The man went down on both knees, his buttocks was sat on his heels. The costumes and the pose, form which it can be estimated that he is a servant. The bottle which was held by the servant, is the winebottle, this type of bottles which was found much in the grave of Jin and Yuan dynasties.

24-2、抱瓶俑（绿衣）

12-13世纪
高15.7厘米

胎色灰黄，质酥松，模制中空，施化妆土，罩透明釉，底无孔。造型是一仆俑抱瓶跪坐，发束双分，两缕头发垂于身前，黑彩涂绘，头顶髡剃，一圈无发，绿彩平涂显示髡剃后的绒发效果。黑彩绘眉眼，身穿束袖绿袍，后背心开光白地画红草花，掩襟，衣领襟半遮于左膝盖。腰系绿革带，背后束扎；带左边悬挂竖囊包，黑彩绘涂红色；带右挂荷包，圆形，黑色涂黄彩，和前述红衣俑一样。右手环屈，左手托抱梅瓶；瓶身黑色口白圈，近口处有黄箍圈；瓶口有孔中空，巧妙的达到俑像烧造透气的效果。双腿跪地，臀压坐脚后跟上。身后的红绿釉彩有明显的过烧痕迹。这两件抱瓶俑，从造型、神态、衣饰明显可以确认是用同一模具模印，仅是主体釉彩一红、一绿的差异。这类成对同模的红绿彩绘俑，甚少见。

24-2. Tomb-figure of man holds bottle (green cloth)

The 12-13th century
Height 15.7cm

The figurine is moulding and hollow, its figuline is lark and loose, daubed the dressing-clay on its body, covered with transparent glaze, the bottom without air-hole. The visual shape which is a servant holds a bottle in his arm and kneels. He's hair divides to either side, two wisps of hair which was painted by black color lolling on the front of body, the calvaria was tonsured with no hair, and laid green color on it to express the effect of down. The child whose eyebrows and eyes was painted with black color, wears green robe with narrow-sleeves, the back was painted red grasses on white background, covered garment's front, the neck-band hangs and covered on the left knee. Ties green hide-band at waist, the back has the knot; at the left side of the waist where was tied a long black bag which painted with red color; at the right side of the waist where was tied black pouch which is nummular, drawn the yellow color, which same as foregoing red cloth tomb-figure. The left arm bent, the right hand held a mei-bottle; the bottle is black with white brim, it has a yellow hoop near the rim; the bottle is hollow, and on its mouth where has a hole to be the airflow orifice for the tomb-figure ingenious. The man went down on both knees, his buttocks was sat on his heels. Its back has the obvious overfired imprint. The two tomb-figures, it can be affirmed that they have the same mold from which visual shape, expression, and costumes, only have the difference in color, one is red, the other is green. This kind of gemeled tomb-figures which have same mold, see little of that.

25、判官俑

12—13世纪
高16.2厘米

胎灰色，模制，施化妆土，罩透明釉，近足处无釉露胎。釉下黑彩在成坯前绘眉眼、胡须、帽、衣袖、靴子。红彩绘衣袍，绿釉彩点衣上花饰，黑彩涂袖口，釉彩多脱落。此造像为一怀抱"名录"卷轴的判官，头戴软脚幞头，幞头上涂抹黄彩，浓须长髯，面涂绿彩，黑釉彩点睛，黄釉彩涂色，立于四方台座上。四方台座底中心处有一透气孔。此造像应该属于玩偶，同样造型的图像，在今天山西保存的宋、金、元庙宇壁画中经常可以看到。

25. The official figurine

The 12-13th century
Height 16.2cm

The figuline is grey, moulding, daubed dressing-clay on the body, and then covered the transparent glaze, close to the foot where it hasn't glaze bared roughcast. The official's eyebrows, eyes, beard, hat, sleeves, and boots were all painted with black color under glaze before the figurine to be semifinished product. The gown was painted with red color, and stippled curlicue with green glaze on it, painted black color on cuffs, most of these colors are discolored. The figurine's shape is an official who carries a scroll "Ming Lu" in his arms, wears Pu Tou (one of man's headgear in antiquity) which was daubed with yellow color, bushy beard and long whiskers, daubed green color on the face, stippled black color on the eyeballs, painted yellow glaze, standing on the square block. There has an air hole in the middle of the square block. The figurine should be part of the toy figurine, the same shape of this figurine, which can be seen on the murals of the temples of Song, Jin, and Yuan Dynasty in Shanxi where has been conserved to this day.

26、夜叉立俑

12—13世纪
高16.8厘米

　　胎色灰黄，模制中空，施化妆土，色白，罩透明釉。造型是一夜叉握拄牙棒立于方台上。绿脸，黄眼，黑睛，红唇，头略斜注视右上方，右肩微耸，头戴黄色角帽，背后红色披发。身穿红色短襦，前襟脱彩，身后红彩鲜艳，挽袖敞怀；下着白裤白鞋，腰系黄带。袖挽露臂，手腕处有黄色箍镯，右手上，左手下，肌肉暴突，交拄黑色牙棒。所露脸、臂、胸、腹皆绿色。夜叉，为佛教护法神"天龙八部"中之一部，梵文为"Yaksa"，夜叉为音译，其意思有"捷疾鬼"、"轻捷"、"勇健"等。《注维摩经》卷一云夜叉有三种："一在地，二在虚空，三天夜叉也。"《法华玄赞》卷二载："夜叉，此云勇健，飞腾空中，摄地行，类诸罗刹也。"佛教以其勇武，而收为护法。此塑像以绿彩涂身，红发披肩，臂腕金环，肌肉暴突，拄握牙棒，生动的表现出了夜叉的勇武。

26. Standing figurine of Yecha (malevolent spirit)

The 12-13th century
Height 16.8cm

The figurine is moulding and hollow, daubed the dressing-clay on its body, color is white, and covered with transparent glaze. The visual shape is a Yecha who holds one tooth-like stick stands on the square platform. Green face, yellow eyes, black eyeballs, and red lips, tilted his head left stares at upper right, and raised his right shoulder slightly, one yellow cuspate cap, disheveled red hair. Wore red short Ru (jacket) which forepart's color has fading, the red color of its back is bright-colored, the front of this clothing is open, rolled up sleeves; white trousers, white shoes, tied a yellow belt at the waist. Rolled the sleeves up bared the arms, the yellow bracelets around both wrists, learned on the tooth-like stick by hands, right is up, left is down, muscularity. The bare face, arms, chest, and belly are all green. Yecha, one of the ghosts in "Tian Long Ba Bu (safeguarding power of Buddha)" the Guardian Deity in Buddhism, the Sanskrit is "Yaksa", Yecha is the transliteration, it has the means "quickly spirit", "nimble", "brave and strong" etc. It was recorded that the Yecha has three kinds that are "one is on the ground, two is in the sky, three is Yecha over the sky" in the vol.1 of ZHU WEI MO JING (ANNOTATION OF THE MAHAYANA SCRIPTURE). The FA HUA XUAN ZAN (SADDHARMAPU. N.DARIKA'S COMMENTARY), of which the vol.2 recorded that "Yecha, brave and strong, flying in the sky, like walking on ground, is similar to Raksa." The Buddhism made him do the Guardian Deity as his valorous. This man of the figurine who has the green body, red hair, gold bracelets, and muscularity, learned on the tooth-like stick, the valorous was shown off dramatically.

27、太上老君像

12—13世纪
高29.8厘米

胎色灰黄质酥松，模制中空，施化妆土，罩透明釉，器底有透气孔。造型为一老翁坐于石台上。头顶梳双髻，黑彩绘眉眼，颔下长髯。身着黄领绿色广袖袍，身后无彩，袖边黑色，腰束黄带，前扎结，两垂带置于腿间；下着白裤，有束腿，黑鞋；两腿交叉。肩有红色绿羽毛云头形披肩，脱色。左手屈举，似拈胡髯；右手五指张开，扶按右腿。就此像之造型神态处理，可以确认其应为道教神祇"太上老君"，老君就是老子，道教尊神。《史记·老子、韩非列传》："老子者，楚苦县厉乡曲仁里人也，姓李氏，名耳。"《神仙传》卷一："老子者……母怀之七十二年乃生。生时剖母腋出，生而白首，故谓老子。……生而能言，指李树曰'以此为我姓'。"因其以李为姓，故唐国公李渊替隋后，就以老子为尊，全面推行道教，这一中国本土宗教，在唐王室的推崇下，取得巨大发展。就图述这件老君像而言，可以确认在12世纪间道教也得到了全面的发展推广，并广受百姓膜拜供奉。

27. The figurine of Laotse

The 12-13th century
Height 29.8cm

The figurine is moulding and hollow, its figuline is lark and loose, daubed the dressing-clay on its body, covered with transparent glaze, and an air-hole on the bottom. The visual shape is an old man sits on the stone platform. Hair worn in double buns, painted black eyebrows and eyes and long beard under chin. Wore green robe which has yellow collar and wide sleeves, the back without color, the sleeves' border is black, yellow belt at the waist front of which was tied a knot and hung between the legs; white trousers, bound shanks, black shoes; crossed his legs. There has the red shawl which is cloud-head shape with green feathers pattern, color is fading. Bent his left hand to pick up the beard; splayed right palm out pressed on the right leg. From this figurine's visual shape, it can be affirmed that the old man is "Tai Shang Lao Jun (Laotse)" the deity of Taoism, Laojun is Laozi, the deity of Taoism. The SHI JI LAOZI HANFEI LIE ZHUAN recorded that "Laozi, who is the people of Qurenli at Lixiang of Chuku country, surname is Li, first name is Er". The vol. 1 of SHEN XIAN ZHUAN (IMMORTAL BIOGRAPHY) recorded that "Laozi, whose mother had conceived him for seventy-two years. He was born from his mother's o armpit, white hair as soon as he was born, so called him old-child (laozi). He could speak as soon as he was born, pointed the Li-tree (plum-tree) and said 'that to be my surname'". Because his surname is Li, so that Li Yuan who is the Guogong of Tang took Laozi as the man of worship, pushed the Taoism across-the-board, Taoism, the Chinese indigenous religion which was held in esteem under Tang's household had gained the tremendous development. From this Laojun figurine, it can be affirmed that the Taoism had gained the development in the period of the 12th century, and was prostrated widely by common people.

28、佩刀吏像

12—13世纪
高23.3厘米

胎色灰黄质酥松，模制中空，施化妆土，色发黄，罩透明釉，器底有透气孔。一吏佩刀立于台座上。头戴黑色包巾，顶有结，黑彩绘眉眼，鼻及额下有短髯，双鬓有垂发。衷衣绿领，束服黑线涂黄；外罩红色绿花翻领袍，多脱色；穿白底黑靴。腰有绿色束带，带中间三个黄色圆饰。双手抱拳作揖。左腋下腰间系带上佩刀，刀首呈如意头，圆镡，涂黄色；刀身有弧线。此种刀式，多见于宋元时期。

28. The figurine of official with walking saber

The 12-13th century
Height 23.3cm

The figurine is moulding and hollow, its figuline is lark and loose, daubed the dressing-clay on its body, color is yellowish, covered with transparent glaze, and an air-hole on the bottom. An official, who wears the saber standing on the block, wears black scarf which has the knot on the top, black eyebrows and eyes, short beard under the nose and chin, lolled hair on each temple. The underclothing has green collar, bound-clothing has yellow pattern which was drawn the black lines; the outer garment is a red robe which has lapel and green flowers pattern, most color had faded; worn the black boots with white soles. Green band around the waist, adorned three yellow rounds in the middle. Both hands made a bow with hands folded in front. At the left of the waist where has a saber, the saber head is Ruyi shape, round saber nose, colored yellow; the saber body has arc. This style of saber was more in the period of Song and Yuan dynasties.

29、醉卧俑

12—13世纪
横长10.8厘米 高7厘米

　　胎色灰黄，模制中空，
施化妆土，罩透明釉。造型
是一文吏卧伏。头戴黑色软
脚幞头，黑彩绘眉眼，面颊
用粉色晕染。着绿袍，袖口
黑色，腰系红色革带，足蹬黑鞋。文吏伏卧，双手交袖，中有孔，达到烧造透气的效果。左侧身
下压一红色圆鼓。就整个人物处理造型的分析，此俑样式很可能出自"太白醉酒"的典故。

29. The tomb-figure of lay for pissed

The 12-13th century
Length 10.8cm, height 7cm

　　The figurine is moulding and hollow, its figuline is lark, daubed the dressing-clay on its body, and covered with transparent glaze. The visual shape is a civil official lay prone. Wore black Putou with soft-horns, the eyebrows and eyes were drown by black color, the cheeks was dyed incarnadine. Green robe, black cuffs, the waist was tied a red hide-belt, wore the black shoes on the feet. The civil official lay prone, put both hands inside the other sleeves, and a hole in the middle to be the airflow orifice. There has a red roundish drum under his left side. Analysed it from the visual shape, the style of this tomb-figure was rooted from the literary quotation of "Tai Bai Zhui Jiu (Taibai drunk)" in all probability.

30、童子捕雀假山摆件

12—13世纪
高21厘米　横宽14.6厘米

　　胎色灰黄质酥松，模制中空，施化妆土，色白，罩透明釉。造型为两个童子玩戏于假山之下。假山造型秀美，黑彩勾山石轮廓和石窝，主体色白，石窝及山石有绿、红、黄釉勾描涂抹，显示山石的苔藓及阴阳效果。山石背后全用黑彩涂绘斜条纹，成石纹肌理。假山右侧角下，坐一孩童，黑彩绘眉眼，红彩点唇，头上额顶一个黑发鬏，系红绳，头顶其他部分绿彩涂抹显示绒发效果，面颊用粉色晕染成皮肤色。穿绿色半臂，领口红色，袖口黄边，手腕戴黄镯；衣服背后画红色开光圈，白地草叶纹。下着粉裤，黑鞋。孩童叉腿，右手屈举，用手背揉右眼，抹泪，怀里抱黑栏绿彩鸟笼，左手扶笼；笼门洞开为孔，巧妙的实现了陶瓷烧造透气孔的效果。孩童脚前有躺置的鸟笼门斜格插板。假山左侧，有另一年龄略大的孩童，攀爬。黑彩绘眉眼，红彩点唇，面颊用粉色晕染成皮肤色，头顶发饰为"鹁角"，三个抓鬏，红色系绳，头顶其他部分绿彩涂抹显示绒发效果。穿绿色半臂，领边、袖口红色，手腕戴黄镯；衣服背后画红色开光圈白地红点。下着粉裤；后腰有遮裙，黄地红边，裙上有五朵红绿花圈；穿黑鞋。头微仰，注视右上方，左手上举攀扣山石，右手上举前探；在右手上方不远处山石上，有一只黄雀正准备往石窝里钻。这只黄雀应该是从下面山脚孩童所抱的笼中飞出，正因为黄雀脱笼，所以小童哭涕。大童攀爬就是为了捕捉黄雀。一幅生动的童戏场景被陶瓷工匠完美的表现出来。这类明显仅有摆设陈列功能的彩绘陶瓷雕塑制品的出现，对当时市民生活的艺术欣赏化有极其重要的研究价值。此无疑是陶瓷制品从日用生活化、宗教信仰化向陈设欣赏化转变的重要标志。

30. Fowling children rockery ornament

The 12-13th century
Height 21cm, width 14.6cm

　　The figurine is moulding and hollow, its figuline is lark and loose, daubed the dressing-clay on its body, color is yellowish, covered with transparent glaze. The visual shape is two children played at the rockery's foot. The shape of rockery is elegant, drew the contour and outline of stone holes with black color, the main part is white color, stone holes and stones were stippled by green, red, and yellow glaze, that to be shown the lichens and the effect of Yin and Yang. The rockery's back was drawn stripes by black color, to be the texture of the stone. At the right of rockery's foot where sat a child, black eyebrows and eyes, red lips, one black Jiu (hair bun) which was tied red taenia on top of the head, and applied viridescent color on the other part expressed the down, the cheeks was dyed incarnadine. Wore the green half sleeves clothing, red collar, yellow cuffs, and wore yellow bracelets on the wrists; drew a red circle in which has grass-blade pattern on the white background at the clothing's back. Incarnadine trousers, black shoes. This child crossed his legs, lifted and bent right arm, rubbed right eye with the hand's back to wipe the tears, clutched a birdcage which is green with black palisade to his bosom, put left hand on the cage; used the cage-door as the air hole to be the airflow orifice for the ceramic fired. At the front of this child's feet, there has the cage-door flashboard, which was laid flatwise with grillwork pattern.
At the left side of rockery, where has an older child shinnying. Painted black eyebrows and eyes, stippled red lips, the cheeks was dyed incarnadine, the hairstyle is "Bo Jiao", three hair-buns, red taenias, applied viridescent color on the other part expressed the down. Wore the green half sleeves clothing, red collar, red cuffs, and wore yellow bracelets on the wrists; drew a red circle in which has red spot pattern on the white background at the clothing's back. Incarnadine trousers; at back of the waist where has covered-skirt, yellow background and red border, five red and green flower-patterns on the skirt; black shoes. Raised his head to stare at upper right, lifted both hands to clamber the stone; on the stone where near the right hand has a yellowbird who is ready to get into the stone-hole. The yellowbird should be the one which flew off from the birdcage that was held by the other child, this child is crying just because the yellowbird escaped from the cage. The older child is clambering to catch this yellowbird. A dramatic scene of playing child was shown by ceramic craftsman. This kind of colored drawing sculpture which only is the ornament without practicability, which has the most important value to research the art taste of the plebes' life at that time. It is the important sign that ceramics changed from commodity and ware for faith to the art ornament.

31、辫发舞蹈俑

12—13世纪
高31.9厘米

　　胎色灰黄，模制中空，施化妆土，罩透明釉，器底有透气孔。造型为一舞者在方台上跳舞。方台黑彩勾框分两层，最底层四面黑点绘涂，形成壶门效果。舞者黑彩绘眉眼，红彩点唇，眉间额头有红彩点靥。发两分，梳双辫，辫梢有绿结带捆扎，垂于身前，头顶髡剃，无发。身着红色黄边绿袖飞雁纹偏襟袍，袍全红，袖及前身藤黄彩绘飞雁，背后无图案。肩披如意形"云肩"，四片，黑红彩勾边，前脸及双肩绿色，背后白色无彩。腰系鞊鞢带，带间装饰绿黄隔片；右腰处带扣上挂黑色白边黄线荷包，荷包上有黄色扎结，绿带。脚穿黑靴。舞者，头微歪，身躯扭转，左手屈腕提甩白巾，右手背腰后甩白巾；双脚交错拧转。巧妙清晰的展现了，12世纪前后戏曲舞蹈的装束与姿态，是难得的戏曲研究材料。在河南省焦作地区的金元墓葬中出土有灰陶跳舞砖雕，其姿态与此相近。

31. Pigtailed Dancer tomb-figure

The 12-13th century
Height 31.9cm

　　The figurine is moulding and hollow, its figuline is lark, daubed the dressing-clay on its body, covered with transparent glaze, and an air-hole on the bottom. The visual shape is a dancer dances on the square platform. This square platform has two layers partitioned by black lines, the four sides of ground layer was drawn by black spots, which form to the effect of Kunmen. The dancer, black eyebrows and eyes, red lips, red Ye (ornament on the face) on the glabella. Combed the hair two parts, two plaits which were tied green taenia at the plaits' end lolling on the front, his calvaria was tonsured without hair. Wore the red robe which has yellow border, green sleeves, flying wild goose patterns, the sleeves and the front were painted gamboge flying wild goose, the back hasn't patterns. Draped "Yun Jian (cloud-shape shawl)" over his shoulders which has four pieces, drew the border by black and red color, its front and double shoulders are green color, the back is white no colors. Tied hide-belt which was decorated with green and yellow parting pieces around waist; at the right of waist where was hang a pouch, the pouch is black with white border and yellow lines, yellow knot on it, green rope. Black boots on feet. The dancer, head sideways, twisted his body, left hand bent and swung a white towel, right hand swung white towel at the back; the two feet are stagger. It was exhibited vividly that the costumes and the posture about the traditional opera dance around the 12th century, is the uncommon material to research the traditional opera. There has one gray-pottery brick-carving with dancer pattern which was unearthed from the grave of Jin to Yuan period in the Jiaozuo area of Henan province, the dancer's posture same as this figure's.

32、招财使者像

12—13世纪
高21厘米

胎色灰黄，模制中空，施化妆土，罩透明釉，器底有透气孔。造型是一男人抱莲花荷叶牌站立石台上。黑彩绘眉眼，短胡须，红彩点唇。黑色发罩，顶有黄箍圈，脖戴十字花黄色项饰，手腕有黄手镯。红色黄点花披帛从颈后腋下穿绕，垂身体两侧。上身无衣；白裤，外罩绿色"合曼"，黄色红圈花带束扎，腰系淡绿红圈花巾；脚蹬红边黑靴。面颊及露肤处用粉色晕染成皮肤色。左手下垂托抱"莲花荷叶牌"，右手屈臂按扶。牌子黑彩绘轮廓线，下底画红色莲花，上顶覆绿色荷叶，牌中框内红彩书写"招财神"。人物环眼、肥脸、短须，似胡人形象。中国古代自古就有财神信仰，如"比干"、"范蠡"、"赵公明"、"关云长"都被视为不同的财神。五代、宋以后财神信仰更被百姓广泛接受，信众如云。在膜拜财神时，主神两侧还有两个供养，左为招财使者，右为利市仙官。百姓甚至直接使用"招财利市"做吉语来祈求金钱财富。现图示这尊塑像应该就是"招财使者"。

32. Messenger of wealth figurine

The 12-13th century
Height 21cm

The figurine is moulding and hollow, its figuline is lark, daubed the dressing-clay on its body, covered with transparent glaze, and an air-hole on the bottom. The visual shape is one man holds a tablet which with lotus-flower and lotus-leaf stands on the stone platform. Painted the eyebrows and eyes with black color, short beard, and stippled lips with red color. Wore black headcloth top of which has yellow ring, yellow pendant which with cross-shaped decoration on neck, and yellow bracelets around his wrists. Draped a red silk-ribbon which with yellow flower-patterns over his shoulders, the silk-ribbon wrapped from neck's back under the both armpits, lolling at the body's both sides. There has no clothing at the upper part of the body; white trousers outside which is green "He Man (one of the clothing)" was tied by the yellow broad belt with red circle flower-patterns, tired viridescence ribbon which with the pattern of red circle and flower at the waist; wore the red border black boots on feet. The cheeks and all bare skin were dyed incarnadine. The "lotus-flower and lotus-leaf tablet" was held in his left hand, and bent right hand to support it. The tablet which was drown the black contour lines, red lotus-flower at the fundus, green lotus-leaf which covered on the top, and red Chinese characters "Zhao Cai Shen" inside the frame. This man has conglobate eyes, fat face, and short beard, like a Huren (Tartars, Mongols, or foreigner). The Mammon religion came up into being in ancient times of China, for example, "Bi Gan", "Fan Li", "Zhao Gongming", and "Guan Yunchang", who were all regarded as the different Mammons. The Mammon religion was accepted abroad by common people since the Five Dynasties and Song Dynasty, the believers is numerous. It still has two Gongyang (figures which were offered in worship) at the both sides of the central figure when worshipped the Mammon, the left is Messenger of wealth, and right is immortal official of good fortune. The common people even used "Zhao Cai Li Shi (bring in wealth and riches)" to pray the money and wealth. This figurine should be the "Messenger of wealth".

33、财神俑

12-13世纪
高22.6厘米

灰胎，模制，施化妆土，罩玻璃釉，少开片。黑彩绘眉、眼、胡须和盔的轮廓。武士头顶的凤翅盔黄、绿、红彩点缀，盔顶有珠。卧蚕眉、丹凤眼、枣红脸、阔口白齿、浓须长髯，大耳垂肩，耳后有红色垂缨。着绿色红黄彩轮状袍，腹部红彩藤黄花"围肚"，系黄色软巾，腰扎革带。右手按单盘腿的膝部，左手抱一只红嘴黄毛长尾鼬（俗称黄鼠狼）。就此造像的体貌特征看，和书中描绘的"关羽"一样。一般情况下，中国人都把"关羽"作为"武圣"忠义的象征来供养膜拜。后敬其信义，世俗逐步以其做"武财神"供奉。华北地区的民间传说中，将狐仙（狐狸）、黄仙（黄鼠狼）、白仙（刺猬）、柳仙（蛇）、灰仙（老鼠），并称（狐黄白柳灰）（或称「灰黄狐白柳」）五大仙，这五仙也称仙家，老百姓常以其为求财之仙，视为财神。其中排名第二的黄鼠狼，百姓俗称其"黄二大爷"。把这个"黄仙"清晰的描绘到关王手中，明确地表示此偶像的"财神"身份。《古今图书集成·神异曲》卷三十七载：北宋宣和五年（1123年）敕封关羽并"令从祀武成王庙"看，宣和五年前关羽就应该以偶像形式享受香火祭祀了。《夷坚志》甲·卷九"关王幞头"条载：潼州关王庙的偶像灵异之事。《夷坚志》丙·卷十"公安药方"条载：向友正，淳熙八年（1181年）为江陵支使，摄公安令，有病，得梦仙人获救。"后诣玉泉祷雨，瞻亭中关王像，盖所感梦者，因绘事于家"。这些记载都证明，关王偶像的崇拜在宋间已经非常流行了。西藏密宗佛教中，有一位名为"藏拉色波"的护法神祇，他就是人们常言的"黄财神"，乃藏密五财神之首，被藏传佛教各大教派普遍供养。在关于他的造像中，每每可以看到他手中捏着一只低头吐物的鼬鼠，这只鼬名字叫"吐宝鼠鼬"（梵文：nakula；藏文：Nevu-le），它吐出珠宝雨，代表无尽的财富。这种鼠鼬吐宝的习俗在中亚地区广为流传。因而不难发现，图录中这尊"关羽"像手中托抱的也可以视为"吐宝鼠鼬"，制作者明确传达了"财神"的信息。这种12-13世纪的中原神祇造像中出现和藏地风格的宗教形式相似的题材，令人关注。由此可见中原地区和西部高原的文化交流，早在12世纪间就已经开始，并且相互影响包容，渗入对方的艺术宗教生活之中。

33. The God of Wealth figurine

The 12-13th century
Height 22.6cm

The figuline is grey, moulding, daubed dressing-clay on the body, and then covered the transparent glaze, few cracked glaze. It was painted the eyebrows, eyes, beard, and helmet's outline with black color. The phoenix-wing helmet was interspersed with yellow, green, and red colors, and there has an orb on the top of helmet. Wocanmei (eyebrows that have the shape of a reclining silkworm), phoenix eyes, jujube red face, big mouth and white teeth, bushy beard and long whiskers, shoulder-length big ears behind which there have red tassels. Wears the grown which decorated with green background red and yellow round flowers, and wears the "Wei Du (cummerbund)" which decorated with red background gamboges flowers on the belly, tied a piece of yellow cloth, and tied leather belt on the waist. The right hand pressed the knee of the right leg which was tucked up, held a weasel (yellow weasel) which has long tail, red mouth, and yellow fur in the left arm. From the bodily appearance of this figurine, it looks like "Guan Yu" described in books. Accustomed, Chinese always look on "Guan Yu" as the "Wu Sheng" who is a loyal and righteous person to worship. Then it was regarded as an especial form of "Wu Caishen (Martial God of Wealth)" to worship, which showed the respect to his good faith. In the folklore at the area of north China, the Hu spirit (fox), Huang spirit (weasel), Bai spirit (hedgehog), Liu spirit (snake), and Hui spirit (mouse), all of which were called the Five Spirits "Hu Huang Bai Liu Hui" or "Hui Huang Hu Bai Liu", this five spirits also be called Xianjia, which was regarded as the Mammon by common people. The second weasel was called the "Huang Er Da Ye (the second Huang uncle)" by common people. Painted this "Huang Spirit" in Guan's hand clearly, which showed this figurine is "Mammon" demonstrably. The vol.37 of GU JIN TU SHU JI CHENG SHEN YI QU (BOOKS OF ANCIENT AND MODERN INTEGRATION) recorded that appointed Guan Yu and "order him be worshiped in Wucheng King Temple subordinate" in the fifth year of Xuan He North Song (A.D. 1123), so, Guan Yu should be regarded as the fetish to worship before the fifth year of Xuan He. The Jia of vol.9 of YI JIAN ZHI in which the "Guan King's Putou" has the record: some strange things about the graven image of Guan King Temple Tong Zhou. The Bing of vol.10 of YI JIAN ZHI in which the "Gongan Prescription" has the record: Xiang Youzheng, is the Jiangling official in the 8th year of Chun Xi, and also is the Gongan Ling part-time, feel bad, and dream that he was rescued by spirit. "Then go to Yuquan to pray rain, look up the figurine of Guan King, like the dream, so painted one in home". These records proved that the Guan King worship had prevailed in the period of Song Dynasty. In the Sitsang Tantra Buddhism, there has one god who protects Buddhism doctrine named "Zang La Se Bo", that who is the common saying "Yellow Jambhala", is the chief of the five Jambhalas, worshiped by all major denominations of Tibetan Buddhism. In about his images, it is often can see a weasel spat out things lower its head, this weasel named "spit treasures weasel" (Sanskrit is nakula, Tibetan is Nevu-le), it spat out things what is endless treasures. It is easy to detect that it is also a "spit treasures weasel" which was held in arm of this "Guan Yu" figurine, the producer want to show us a "God of Wealth" undoubtedly. This religionary modality of the Tibetan style appeared in the wares of the god figurine of central plains. Thus it can be seen that the religionary cultural exchange which between the Central Plains and Western Plateau, had begun as early as the 12th century, mutual influenced and forgave, infiltrated into the life each other.

34、托宝珠坐俑

12—13世纪
高37厘米

胎灰黄色较酥松，模制中空，施化妆土，通体罩透明釉，底部无釉露胎，有透气孔。造型是一武士托珠坐于石台上。黑彩绘短髭、络腮胡，虬眉宽鼻，阔口露齿，唇齿红色。头戴凤翅冠，冠顶红衬绿饰，冠前绿花红珠，冠侧两凤翅黄绿相间，两条黄色淡绿边束冠带垂搭肩头。身着红袍，披绿色红边的如意形"云肩"四片，黑红彩勾边，前脸及双肩绿色，背后白色无彩。腰围绿色红团菊"袍肚"，系黄束带，腰部绿带紧扎"袍肚"。左腿垂立，右腿横屈台座上，红袍下垂半盖腿，露白裤，脚蹬红边白靴。武士左手按胯，右手置右大腿，托绿色红框淡绿边方巾，巾上有宝珠，珠顶云气，绿白相间螺旋上升。就其面貌神态可以基本判定其为胡人。《太平广记》卷四〇三《魏生·出「原化记」》载："尝因胡客自为宝会。胡客法，每年一度与乡人大会，各阅宝物，宝物多者，戴帽居于座上，其余以次分列。"由此不难发现此塑像展示的明显就是"胡客斗宝"。同类胡客展宝塑像，台湾鸿禧美术馆亦有藏，其胡客手中所持为"宝角"，塑像高达50厘米。可能因武士妆束有威仪感，所以在塑形时工匠们借用了，威严的武士衣着外形。另就《东京梦华录》中京城（开封）有"祆庙"的记载。疑如此体量的胡客展宝像，与当时的民间祆祠供养有关。此像出土于河南省延津县沙河城地区，12世纪前后黄河北流未南滚，此地在汴梁城北郊。

34. The sitting figurine of man holds the precious-pearl

The 12-13th century
Height 37cm

The figurine is moulding and hollow, its figuline is lark and loose, daubed the dressing-clay on its body, covered with transparent glaze, the bottom which has an air-hole but no glaze on it. The visual shape is one warrior holds a pearl sits on the stone platform. The short mustache and whiskers were drawn by black color, curling eyebrows and wide nose, broad mouth bare teeth, red lips and teeth. He wears the phoenix-wing crest, which has green ornament with red background on its top, green flower red pearl on its front, two phoenix-wings alternated with green and red at its both sides, two pieces of belt which is yellow with viridescent border lolling on the shoulders. He wears the red robe, drapes four pieces of red border green "Yunjian (cloud-shape shawl) over his shoulders, this "Yunjian" was drawn the outline with red and black color, which has green color on its front and double shoulders, but its back is white no colors. He wears green "Baodu" which with chrysanthemums pattern around his waist, ties yellow broad belt, the "Baodu" was fastened by green belt. The left leg hangs, right leg was bent on the platform, the red robe lolls to cover the legs half and bare the white trousers, wears red border white boots. The warrior presses his hip with his left hand, the right hand on his right thigh and holds a piece of green square towel which has red frame and pea green border in his palm, on the towel where has one precious-pearl, it has the cloudy obscured haze which is green and white alternate, climbs gyroidal on the top of the pearl. From his visage, it can be judged basically that he is the Huren. The YUAN HUA JI·WEI SHENG which is the vol.403 of TAI PING GUANG JI (PEACEFUL BROADLY RECORDS) recorded that "The Huren has their own treasure meeting. This meeting is an annual event which with fellow people, view and admire the treasures each other, one man who has the most treasures can wear the crown and sit on the seat, the rest sit by arranged." So it can be found that is "Hu people's treasure contest" from this figurine. The same kind of this figurine, which was also collected by Chang Foundation Taiwan, this figurine is 50 centimeter high, but the treasure which was held by Huren is the "Bao Jiao". The craftsmen borrowed the warrior's clothing style and externality when made this kind of figurines, maybe because the style of warrior's dressing has the impressive manner. Furthermore, the DONG JING MENG HUA LU (RECOLLECT THE FLOURISHING DONGJING.) recorded that it has the "Zoroastrianism Temple" in the capital (Kaifeng). This size of the Huren figurine should have the relations with offered in worship to Zoroastrianism Temple. The figurine was unearthed in the Shahecheng area of Yanjin Xian in Henan Province, this place at the north suburb of the city Bianliang.

35-1、"秦叔宝"像

12—13世纪
高41.5厘米   底座长16厘米   宽10.5厘米

　　胎灰黄色较酥松，模制，施化妆土，通体罩透明釉，底部无釉露胎，有2.5厘米左右的椭圆形透气孔。造型是一右手握剑柄，左手握剑尖，短髭、垂须、浓眉，龙鼻凤眼，目光正视前方，气度非凡的武士站立于石台之上。武士头戴凤翅盔，盔顶有红缨，披黄色绿边的"披肩"，身着白色战袍，两肩披搭红色加黄蔓草纹的"披帛"直垂及脚下。小臂套有绿色开光的红花"护臂"，上衣为红色"米字田格锦地纹"。腰围黑边黄色"袍肚"，"袍肚"又名"抱肚"、"包肚"乃宋、金、元时期常见的腰部用饰，开始仅为武士使用，属戎服，后来则文武兼用，颜色由朝廷颁赐（见：《宋史·舆服志》）。元代称为"捍腰"，至明朝时仍然流行。腰有系带紧扎"袍肚"。白袍下垂盖腿，露白裤，有红带扎小腿，脚蹬黑靴，腰前有两条绿色垂缘。此样式属于中国古代儒雅武将的造型，在墓道门俑、寺庙山门、神仙水陆卷轴画及家用门神画中都有出现，使用的非常广泛。中国人对这类武士的描摹就希望借此武将获得平安的守护。

35-1. The "Qin Shubao" figurine

The 12-13th century
Height 41.5cm, Length of the pedestal 16cm, Width 10.5cm

Yellow figuline is loose, moulding, daubed dressing-clay, and then covered with transparent glaze, and the base is bare without glaze on where has an elliptic air hole about 2.5 centimeters. This figurine is a warrior who has extraordinary bearing, short moustache, unbent whiskers, dense eyebrows, dragon-nose, and phoenix-eyes that stared straight ahead, held sword-handle in right hand, the left hand held sword-tip, stood on a stone platform. The warrior wears a phoenix-wing helmet, on top of which it has red tassel, drapes a "Pi Jian (a shawl)" which is yellow and with green border over his shoulders, wears white campaign gown, and drapes the "Pi Bo (silk ribbon)" which is red background yellow pattern of tendril over two shoulders down to the feet. The lower arms were covered with "Hu Bi (arm shield)" which are green background red flowers, the upper outer garment has the pattern of red "brocade background with checked". The waist was wrapped with black border yellow "Pao Du", "Pao Du" also named "Bao Du", which was the common decoration of waist at the dates of Song, Jin, and Yuan dynasties, and only for the warrior was the martial attire at the very start, in the sequel, it was not only for the warrior but also for civilian, what color was distributed by imperial government (see: SONG SHI·YU FU ZHI (HISTORY OF SONG·RECORD OF VEHICLE CLOTHES AND HAT). It was called "Han Yao (waist guard)" at Yuan Dynasty, it was still prevalent in Ming dynasty. It has a belt fastened the "Pao Du" at the waist. The white gown drooped covered legs, bared the white trousers which were tied with red riband under the knees, wears black boots on feet, two green silk ribbons hang at the front of waist. The mode of this figurine is the appearance of Chinese hoary cultured military officer, it was used widely, appeared in the path of tomb, the tomb figure, the temple, the temple gate, scroll drew with supernatural being, and door-god painting. Chinese people drew this kind of warriors to wish under the guardianship of the military officer.

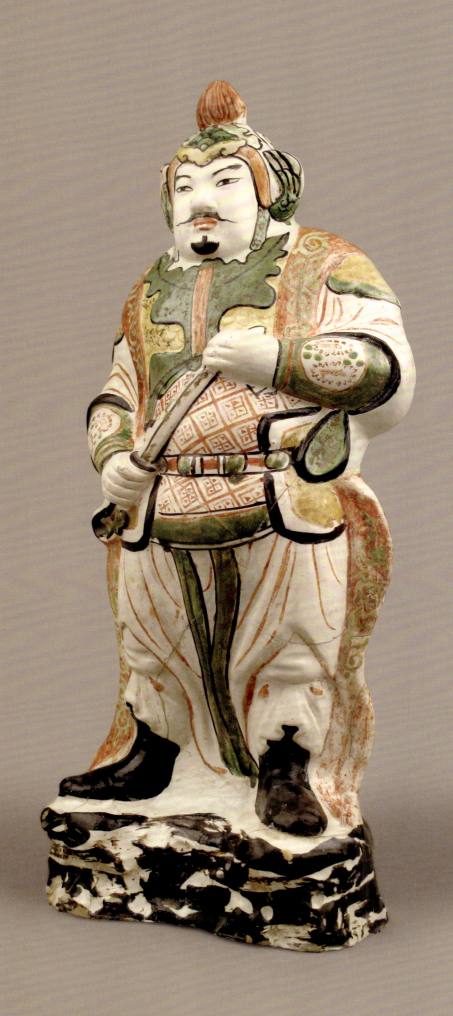

35-2、"程咬金"像

12—13世纪
高40.5厘米　底座长15.5厘米　宽10厘米

胎灰黄色较酥松，模制，施化妆土，通体罩透明釉，底部无釉露胎，有2.3厘米左右的椭圆形透气孔。造型是一左手握斧柄，右手拳握、短髭、络腮胡长髯剑眉，宽鼻阔口环眼，目视左下方，威风凛凛的武士站立于石台之上。武士头戴云月盔，披绿色黄边的"披肩"，身着大红战袍，两肩披搭白色"披帛"直垂及脚下，有螺旋卷纹。小臂套有黄色开光的小红碎花"护臂"，上身着绿被襟黄色菱钉重甲，腹部有护心镜，腰围红边白色"袍肚"，系回纹绿点带紧扎"袍肚"。黑边大红袍下垂盖腿，露白裤，有红带扎小腿，脚蹬白靴，腰前有两条黄色垂缘。它和上图应该属于同一组俑像，非常近似于从唐代开始流传的护卫武士"秦叔宝"、"程咬金"的造型，它们有时也被借用为佛教的护法天王。此同样造型的武士俑河北彭城地区有出土，高34厘米（见：《中国陶瓷史》图版贰拾柒3）。

35-2. The "Cheng Yaojin" figurine

The 12-13th century
Height 40.5cm, Length of the pedestal 15.5cm, Width 10cm

Yellow figuline is loose, moulding, daubed dressing-clay, and then covered with transparent glaze, and the base is bare without glaze on where has an elliptic air hole about 2.5 centimeters. This figurine is a warrior who is commanding, short moustache, a heavy whiskers, long beard, dashing eyebrows, wide nose, big mouth, round eyes, looked down to the left, held an axe with long handle in left hand, stood on a stone platform. The warrior wears a helmet decorated with clouds and crescent moon patterns, drapes a "Pi Jian (a shawl)" which is green and with yellow border over his shoulders, wears bright red campaign gown, and drapes the white "Pi Bo (silk ribbon)" over two shoulders down to the feet, The lower arms were covered with "Hu Bi (arm shield)" which are yellow background with scattered red small flowers, wears heavy armor which has green background with yellow rivets, a round-shaped breast protector of armor on the abdomen, wraps white "Pao Du" with red border around the waist, It has a belt which has the fret pattern and with green rings fastened the "Pao Du" around the waist. The black border bright red gown drooped covered legs, bared the white trousers which were tied with red riband under the knees, wears white boots on feet, two yellow silk ribbons hang at the front of waist. It with the figurine above should be the same set of figurines, are very similar to the figure which are the bodyguard warrior "Qin Shubao" and "Cheng Yaojin" circulated from Tang Dynasty, sometimes, they were borrowed to be the gods who protect Buddhism doctrine. The same figurine also is unearthed at Peng Cheng of Hebei province, height is 34 centimeters (see: HISTORY OF CHINESE CERAMICS, the plate 27-3).

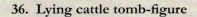

36、卧牛俑

12—13世纪
宽16厘米　高9.5厘米

　　胎色灰黄，模制中空，施化
妆土，底有透气孔。造型为一只牛
伏卧于椭圆台上，牛头上仰，口微
张。牛身柿红色，角白；尾摆于左侧，椭圆台局部抹绿彩。整个牛的塑形神态生动传神。此牛原
本应该是黑釉的，在黑釉上又加罩矾红二次烤花，才呈现柿红色。后加彩笔触在牛角、耳、尾处
能看到痕迹。此类标准的柿釉（也称酱釉）制品在定窑、当阳峪窑、耀州窑等都有烧造，但成色
原理不同。而如此黑釉加矾红二次烤花的柿色制品，目前已知存世的仅此一件。

36. Lying cattle tomb-figure

The 12-13th century
Width 16cm, height 9.5cm

　　The figurine is moulding and hollow, its figuline is lark, daubed the dressing-clay on its body, and an air-hole on the bottom. The visual shape is a cattle lies on the elliptical platform, raises its head, and opens mouth. The cattle's body is persimmon-red (crimson), horns are white; its tail was placed at the left side, the elliptical platform was daubed green color at the parts. It is vivid that the figure of this cattle. This cattle should be black originally, it was covered the Fanhong (one of red color of glaze) on the black glaze and then fired second for decorating fire to appear the persimmon-red color. We can found the trace of adding color on the cattle's horns, ears, and tail. This kind of normal Shi (persimmon) glaze (also called Jiang glaze, color is dark reddish brown) wares, which were fired at Ding Kiln, Dangyangyu Kiln, Yaozhou Kiln, etc, bur the elements about color are different. This Shi glaze ware which was covered Fanhong on the black glaze and then fired second for decorating fire, is the only one in actual existence.

Postscript

The sixty years is a cycle, the thirty years is a generation.

2009, is the 60th birthday of our great motherland. Chinese people never like today that not only travels proudly all over the world, but also shows our bran-new elegant demeanour. The Chinese nation proclaims that she stands firm among the nations of the world with her own strong vitality and creativity. Today, the "made in China" could already be seen in every corner of the world, tomorrow, the "created in China" shall be concerned by the whole world.

At a thousand years ago, China—china, which became the most valuable treasure for the foreign lands, along with the voice of the sea under the seagoing vessels, and the voice of the camel bell on Silk Road. The "created in China" is the rare treasures admired by the whole world. We recall the past in the light of the present, admire the Chinese ancestors gained so great achievements, and feel the new China have paid the toil for these 60 years.

On the occasion of 2009, that is the PRC's 60th anniversary. Thanks for the help from Shenzhen Municipal Committee and Government leaders, craft brother and every prominent personage, to give us this chance to show our humble museum's the most precious collections, and offer our the most sincere congratulations to our great motherland!

These rare collections with a history of more that 800 years, she, is the multi-color overglaze painted ceramic which was seen the first by all mankind, it opened a colorful ear for the Chinese ceramics history and even the World ceramics history. Her achievements brought the huge revolution to the human society, no less than the TV from black and white to color. As a result of the haste, pick these 36 pieces (groups) of figurines to press, first. With the compliments!

Finally, thank the Minister Wang Jingsheng for taking time off his busy schedule to write the preface, thank the Special Fund of Development of the Propagandize and Cultural Undertakings of Shenzhen for aiding financially, thank the Shenzhen Bureau of Cultural Relics, Shenzhen Museum, Shenzhen Office of Cultural Relics Management, and Shenzhen School of Cultural Relics Archaeology and Appraisal for all-out supporting, and thank the numerous preeminently talented persons for helping. We feel grateful to offer best wishes!

Splendid·China! China·Splendid!

Shenzhen Wangye Museum
September 2, 2009

后 记

六十年一个甲子，三十年一世人。

2009年，伟大的祖国，六十岁生日。中国人从来没有像今天这样可以自豪的走遍全世界，同时也向世界展示自己的全新风采。中华民族以自己强大的生命力和创造力，向世人宣告其昂首屹立于世界民族之林。今天中国制造已经可以在世界的每一个角落被看到，明天中国创造必将被全世界关注。

一千多年前，中国——陶瓷，随着海船下的涛声，丝路上的驼铃，成为异域民族追捧的至宝。中国创造是全世界羡慕的奇珍。抚今追昔，钦佩华夏先人取得的伟大成就，同时感慨新中国六十年付出的艰忍辛劳。

藉此2009年中华人民共和国六十周年大庆之际。拜深圳市委及政府领导和各位同行贤达关照，让我们有机会捧上寒馆最珍贵的收藏，向伟大祖国献上我们最真诚的祝贺！

这批珍藏距今已有近800余年，她们是全人类第一次看到的釉上多色彩绘陶瓷，她的出现开启了中国陶瓷史乃至世界陶瓷史的绚丽多彩时代。她的成就不亚于电视从黑白到彩色给人类社会带来的巨大变革。时间仓促，先撷取36件（组）雕塑付梓。谨致敬贺！

最后感谢京生部长政务劳忙之际拨冗致序，感谢深圳市宣传文化事业发展专项基金资助，感谢深圳市文物局、深圳市博物馆、深圳市文管办、深圳市文物考古鉴定所的大力支持和众多社会俊彦的帮助。心怀感激，敬献祝福！

精彩·中国！中国·精彩！

深圳望野博物馆

2009年9月2日

深圳市宣传文化事业发展专项基金资助项目

"精彩·中国——公元12-13世纪彩瓷的辉煌" 展

主　　办：深圳市文物局
承　　办：深圳博物馆
　　　　　深圳望野博物馆
　　　　　深圳市文物管理办公室
　　　　　深圳市文物考古鉴定所
展览策划：尹昌龙　柴凤春　阎　焰
编委主任：杨耀林
编　　委：叶　杨　郭学雷　刘　涛　任志录　阎　焰
图录编著：望　野
统　　筹：郭学雷
摄　　影：安　玲
展　　务：李维学

图书在版编目（CIP）数据

精彩 / 望野编著.–北京：文物出版社，2009.9
ISBN 978–7–5010–2830–6

Ⅰ. 精…　Ⅱ. 望…　Ⅲ.①彩绘–瓷器（考古）–中国–
宋代–图录②彩绘–瓷器（考古）–中国–金代–图录
Ⅳ. K876.32

中国版本图书馆CIP数据核字（2009）第160406号

精彩 / 望野 编著

英文翻译：戴　婵
书籍设计：敬人书籍设计
责任印制：潘拥军
责任编辑：张小舟

出版发行：文物出版社
网　　址：http://www.wenwu.com
E_mail：web@wenwu.com
制版印刷：精一印刷（深圳）有限公司
经　　销：新华书店
开　　本：635×965mm　1/16
印　　张：6.5
版　　次：2009年9月第1版
印　　次：2009年9月第1次印刷
书　　号：ISBN 978–7–5010–2830–6
定　　价：180.00元